About Transform

"I got off anti-depressa.
- Elizabeth B., MSW, Social Worker

"The genius here is in the blending of the conscious and unconscious minds to achieve our highest potential."
- Christopher C. French, MD, MPH

"I had no clue what joy was... Now my life is full of joy and I am losing weight too."
- Elizabeth Comeau

"I kicked a 40+ year cigarette habit... and stopped meat, caffeine and alcohol."
- Tom Kinhan

"In martial arts it helps with focus, ki and strength. Judith Kravitz is an angel and has raised my consciousness and kicks with Transformational Breathing."
- L.A. Bek, Black belt, owner
  Otis Ridge Camp for Martial Arts

"A tool I will use personally and professionally the rest of my life... Patients have reported more energy, and pain relief of all kinds... headaches, low back pain, digestive disturbances."
- Patrick L. Dorman, D.C., Chiropractor

"My breathing is so much freer... layers of stress have melted away. I highly recommend it."
- Enid Zuckerman, Canyon Ranch

"I really trust Judith and Transformational Breathing™."
- Ken Page, founder, Multi-dimensional
  Cellular Healing Institute

"I recommend it to all my clients. It has changed my life."
- Shashi French, D.C., Chiropractor

"Of all the modalities we use, if I had to choose just one, it would be Transformational Breath."
- Janet L. Orion, D.C., Chiropractor

"I have since created a fascinating life of joyful work and play."
- Karen K. Keefe, Ph.D.

"I've known for years that I create my own reality. I just didn't know how to create what I wanted. Now I do. It's very tangible."
- Lois Grasso, OxyGenesis Institute

"Transformational Breathing has blessed me with a dramatic shift in attitude, and gradually lifted the physical accumulation of years of stress, which had caused frequent exhaustion and depression."

- Lisa Clare Kombrink, Town Attorney,
Town of Southampton, New York

"It made me relax and not worry about the little things in life. I never realized how much breathing has to do with you everyday emotions." - Julie S.

"Transformational Breathing cleared much of the anger, the detachment and the sadness. As a matter of fact, it helped me mentally rework my entire philosophy of life."

- Chris Riopelle

" It has helped me to move through a major airplane phobia. I have dropped the use of blood pressure medication, tranquilizers, antacids, etc. My body feels much better than it has since I can remember – stronger and freer. Many emotional blockages and resistances have gone away."

- Gene Troy

"You, like me, can get up off the floor and draw your misplaced power back to yourself. The most empowering work I did for this was the deep breath work."

- Joan Gatuso, *A Course in Life*

"That one breath session was worth more than two years of therapy" - Gabrielle Hass, director of the Blind
Children's Learning Ctr, Tustin, CA

"Approximately ten minutes into the breathing, I envisioned a deep rich cobalt blue. My body and soul melted into color, and I experienced ... the One cosmic consciousness."

- Pamela H., Nov. '98 participant at Owens Retreat

"TB has helped me with my main passion, the Martial Arts.... It makes my performance easier. It has made many things clearer, from the way I see them to the way I deal with them."

- Angie B.

"Breathing gives me the kind of high that music does and snow-boarding – things that I love." - John B.

I dedicate this book to our friend,
Peter Hutchins,
whose passing taught us
so much about the precious
gifts of life and breath.

Breathe Deep, Laugh Loudly: The Joy of Transformational Breathing™

FIRST REVISED EDITION

Revised edition, June 2002
Published by Free Breath Press, PO Box 313 Center Sandwich NH 03227, Telephone: 603.284.9291

Originally published 1999 by INI Free Press, West Hartford CT 06119

LIBRARY OF CONGRESS CATALOGUING IN PUBLICATION DATA
Kravitz, Judith, 1946
    Breathe Deep, Laugh Loudly: The Joy of Transformational Breathing /
Judith Kravitz / 224 pages
ISBN: 1-929271-01-8
CIP: 99-66174
Printed and bound in the United States of America

Typesetting and design by Lois Como-Grasso and Catherine Doucette
Front cover design and artwork by Eric Almaas
Primary editors: Lois Como-Grasso, Laura Jensen, Marilyn Perona

This edition is printed on acid-free paper that meets the American National Standards Institute Z39.48 Standard.

For information about Transformational Breathing™ workshops and the personal and professional training program, contact:
Transformational Breath Foundation
PO Box 313 Center Sandwich NH 03227
Telephone: 603 284 9291
Website: www.breathe2000.com
Email: info@breathe2000.com

Breathe Deep, Laugh Loudly

The Joy of Transformational Breathing

Judith Kravitz

Free Breath Press

About the Author

Judith Kravitz, D.M.

An ordained minister with a Doctorate Degree in Metaphysics, Judith Kravitz has dedicated 30 plus years to raising her children and developing the profound self-healing technology that is now widely renowned and trademarked as Transformational Breathing.

Judith was diagnosed with a cancerous tumor on her neck in 1979. She chose to heal it without drugs or surgery and did so quite successfully with the help of conscious breathing and other self-empowerment practices, which have become the foundation for Transformational Breath training. The mother of eight biological and two step-children, she now enjoys radiant health and five grandchildren as well.

The original co-founder of the International Breath Institute, Judith has since founded the Transformational Breath Foundation, an independent not-for-profit organization based in New Hampshire.

Judith travels extensively across the globe sharing the power of breath through this amazingly transforming technology. Since 1980, she has trained over 3,000 facilitators and several hundred certification trainers. She has personally facilitated breathing sessions for more than 100,000 people in groups and individual sessions. Known as the "breath therapist to the stars," Judith's client list includes many celebrities and some of the most respected leaders of our time.

Acknowledgments

It is with great love and humility that I bring forth the following information with the help of many. First and foremost, I give thanks to the Spirit of All for giving me the gift and experiences of this utterly amazing form of "play" that has come to be known as Transformational Breathing™. In fulfilling a part of my own life's purpose, I am honored to be adding to the body of knowledge pertaining to conscious breathing, thus keeping the practice ever-growing and improving. Through sharing this gift with so many people throughout the world, I have been shown that the breath is our most simple yet powerful tool for joyful healing and passionate living.

There are several individuals whose key contributions and input made this book a reality. Lois Grasso's gift for developing concepts with words brought many ideas to life. There is a synergistic magic between us—words flow, ideas gel, and concepts come together. As primary editor and coordinator, her drive brought this project to fruition. Next, I want to acknowledge Marilyn Perona, whose dedication and hard work were invaluable in the editing of this second edition.

Heartfelt gratitude also goes to those who supported this project with their faith in the form of money, and also to Laura Jensen, Dr. Scott Kwiatkowski, Liz Comeau, Carol Hawk, Cynthia Van Savage, Judy Taché, Catherine Creegan, Catherine Doucette, Kathy Glass, Samvedam Randles, Kevin Macarewicz, Dr. Abraham Sussman, Richard Handel, and "Peaches" Udoma, all of whom contributed their knowledge, talents and experience with genuine dedication and caring for this work. This book is truly a co-creation of loving souls.

Thanks to the talented artist, Eric Almaas, who created the cover, illustrating the beauty of the four elements; to my friend Norman Lear, who continues to support this work in a variety of valuable ways; and to the many wonderful facilitators and clients whose personal sharing breathed true life into these pages.

I deliver this, my "ninth child," to you, the reader, in the faith that you will reclaim your greatest asset: the inherent gift of your own life, laughter, and creativity in every Transformational Breath.

Preface

Over the course of my 28-year professional practice working with more than 100,000 people, both privately and in groups, I have experienced a wide variety of approaches to holistic healing. Nowhere in my travels have I ever seen a therapeutic process that can so readily, reliably, and joyfully free us from the negative conditioning and trauma of the past. Transformational Breathing gives us the power to create healthy, energized, passionate lives.

My first experience of conscious breathing was in the mid-seventies, when I worked with a Rebirther in Sonoma County, California. Rebirthing is a process that utilizes non-stop conscious breathing in hour-long sessions to release trauma sustained at birth. It was quite powerful in my own life: it seemed to take me back in time to clear self-limiting beliefs that began as early as birth. After several rebirthing sessions, my facilitator suggested I incorporate conscious breathing into the healing work I was doing as a counseling minister. I began rebirthing clients in the late seventies. It took my work to a deeper level and in all cases was very beneficial.

Almost immediately after I introduced breath work to my clients, I received insights to make it even more effective, powerful, and lasting. I continued to incorporate information as it came to me, and the response from clients grew ever more gratifying. Soon my work no longer fit the definition of Rebirthing. There had been major changes in the form, consciousness, techniques, and intention of the process. I began calling it Transformational Breathing.

Nearly a year later, I was diagnosed with throat cancer and advised to have the cancer surgically removed. As a health-oriented twenty-nine-year-old with two young children, I was in shock. Surgery did not feel right to me, even though not operating seemed pretty scary. I knew, however, from my metaphysical background and knowledge of breath work, that cancer could be healed. I prayed and asked for direction. The answer I received was quite challenging: I was to heal myself without surgery or drugs. At that point, I realized that all the methods I had learned over the years had led me to this point——if I had the courage to choose that path.

I began to work with the breath even more diligently, finding new insights daily. During one of my breathing sessions, it became vividly clear that I needed to change the way I ate. I began lightening up my diet, eating more fresh fruits and vegetables and eliminating all red meat. Soon I was feeling lighter myself and had more energy than before. In my frequent breathing sessions, flurries of unresolved anger began coming up to be healed. Feelings from early childhood that I had never been free to express surfaced and dissolved with the energy of my own breath. I also felt waves of forgiveness emerging from a very sacred space and filling me with gratitude and joy.

As I continued to gain clarity and faith through the breathing, I found it increasingly important not to focus on the symptoms of the disease, but to affirm and know my innate wholeness and perfection. I trained myself not to examine the growth bulging out of my neck in the mirror, but to pay attention to positive things I could acknowledge about myself. One day, several months after embarking on this self-healing journey, I was putting lotion on my body; when I got to the neck area, I discovered the lump was gone! I knew at that moment I was involved with something miraculous—far beyond my human experience.

Several years after this healing, I felt a strong urge to leave California and raise my young children in a clean, wholesome, country environment. They seemed to be growing up too fast. In the early eighties, we moved our six children (number seven was on the way!) to a small town in Maine.

Compared to California, Maine seemed like another planet. Going from the heart of the holistic health movement to a rural town of five hundred people was quite a culture shock. We were now surrounded by the beauty of Nature, clean air, and open spaces, but there was very little knowledge of self-healing, conscious breathing, or holistic living.

Many times I cried out in despair, "What am I doing here?" I wanted to share the gifts of Transformational Breathing with as many people as possible. I knew that the answers inherent in breathwork ran deep into the soul of humankind, bringing deep peace to those who practiced it. I feared I could never reach enough people if I stayed in Maine.

When I settled down long enough to listen within, however, I received the understanding that I had moved to Maine to continue developing the process with more internal guidance and less exterior influence. It was important to sow the seeds of breath in the fertile hearts of these kind people. I began teaching yoga and meditation classes at the local high school and offering self-awareness groups. I shared the breathing with anyone who seemed open enough to try it. Soon there was enough interest to train a few groups of people to facilitate sessions for others, and the professional certification training began expanding throughout New England.

I have since had the pleasure of training people in numerous cities throughout the United States and Europe, as well as in Latin America, the Middle East, and Asia.

Transformational Breath™ is now a fine-tuned art and science, which can be readily taught and duplicated by all who apply themselves to personal self-healing and proper training. It expands upon the foundations of Leonard Orr's Rebirthing, which brought conscious breathing to people in the Western hemisphere, and shares some fundamentals with Dr. Stanislav Grof's Holotropic Breathwork. My own doctorate degree in the science of metaphysics and blend of experience and training in Kundalini Yoga, sound healing, body mapping, and more, has certainly been instrumental in bringing Transformational Breathing to the forefront of breath work today; however, I truly feel that it is God's gift to the world and I am just the messenger.

It never ceases to amaze me how much love, power, and joy this breathing brings to the lives of those who take it in and play with it. Regardless of color, creed, religion, career, nationality, political beliefs, sexual orientation, physical condition, culture and language—we all get it. No discrimination here; this is an unequaled enjoyment opportunity.

In my experience, only one factor determines the quality of success and amount of permanent joy each of us can experience. That factor is choice. Everyone wants joy and success. Not everyone actively chooses it.

Breathe Deep. Laugh Loudly. Live well. Quality of life relies upon quality of breath. How much joy will you choose?

— Dr. Judith Kravitz

Table of Contents

"Breathe deeply and gently
through every cell of the body.
Laugh happily and release the
head of all worries and anxieties;
and finally breathe in the blessings of
love, hope, and immortality
that are flowing in the air,
and you will understand
the meaning of human breath."

- Pundit Acharya

Part One

"You are asking me for tools,
and I am giving them to you.
Breathe.
Breathe long and deep.
Breathe slowly and gently.
Breathe in the soft, sweet
nothingness of life,
so full of energy, so full of love.
It is God's love you are breathing.
Breathe deeply and you can feel it.
Breathe very, very deeply
and the love will make you cry.
For Joy.
For you have met your God,
and your God has
introduced you to your soul."

Conversations with God:
An Uncommon Dialogue, Book 3
Neale Donald Walsch

"Inner View" of a Breather

On December 5, 1998, Elizabeth Comeau had her first Transformational Breathing session at a training clinic where her sister was being trained for certification. Plagued with severe depression, Liz couldn't even imagine what the word "joy" meant. A single mother in her early thirties, she found despair a far more familiar concept.

In this chapter, "Liz" vividly and courageously recalls the constant stream of fearful thoughts and compulsive, self-sabotaging habits that had gripped her for years. Let's ride with her as she travels to the session and begins a journey so profound that her life would be unrecognizable just two months later. From the depths of depression and despair to the heights of love, power, and joy, this is not an embellished description. This is a true story and, thank God, not a rare one.

Doubt, skepticism, and outright fear cloud my mind as my mom and I set out on this nebulous journey... toward what? Breath? Joy? Peace? Simply obscure mythical dreams to me. Apparently others can experience joy, but this is a completely foreign concept to me. Becoming joyful seems about as plausible as the prospect of becoming anorexic. It just ain't gonna happen. Ice cream and chocolate happen to be my best friends. Is this joy thing going to demand the relinquishment of these pleasures?

But okay, I'm going. I promised my sister—that person I barely know anymore. Gone are the days of decadent food-commiserating-binges in which we once indulged. She will have none of that anymore. She's way too joyful for that nonsense.

She'd rather breathe. Do I resent this? Yes! Now who can I com-plain to about life's many tragedies? Where else will I receive the pity I so desperately seek?

My mother could provide it, but she has such a condescend-ing manner about her. I really can't take much of it. When she pities me, I feel like a pathetic idiot.

She sits next to me now, moaning and groaning in the background about all of life's injustices and terrible drivers and the dirty windshield and—

"What, ma? Yes, I know that the insurance company is raking you over the coals. We've discussed it at least a dozen times. I'm sorry I hurt your feelings, but—WHAT? Yes, I saw that car. Don't worry, I'm in control."

But am I in control? As her verbal miseries fade into dull drone, I ponder the question. It seems the more I strive to control my life, the more chaotic it becomes. Hmmm, let's count the tragedies over the last year or so.

I had bought a business, after receiving a small car accident settlement, because I wanted to have more control over my life. Three months later, I bought my first home (can't stand bosses or landlords) and within a month the business went belly up. Hmm, then what? Months of severe depression, my first new car was repossessed, and I got skunked out of my home.

"Oh! Liz!" Mom is bracing herself firmly between the dash-board and the seat back. Some guy in a big black truck just slammed on his brakes to take a turn with no blinker.

"I got it, ma." Right at home in a crisis, I quickly lay on the horn in a fit of rage. It feels good to yell. "Learn how to drive, you *!?%*!!"

Mother chimes in, whining, "My God, what is wrong with these people? Don't they care if they cause an accident? That jerk!"

"All right, ma, it's over now."

After a variety of skunk remedies that didn't work and two months of virtual homelessness, my ten-year-old son and I are finally living back home. Of course, I can't pay my mortgage and am already behind. The sheriff is expected any day now to throw us out due to foreclosure. Nice Christmas.

Isn't life joyful? Sorry, sis. My reality is doom and despair. Yet, I resent the woman next to me for verbalizing it. I don't really need or want confirmation of my belief that this world is a hellish nightmare. On the other hand, the notion that someone will change that belief by "breathing" me seems utterly ludicrous. What am I, nuts? Taking this four-hour trip across New Hampshire to Vermont?

Yet, what else do I have to do? Sit at home, watch bad TV and wait for the sheriff while eating a half gallon of Breyer's Mint Chocolate Chip? (It *is* all natural, you know.)

As we draw nearer to the clinic, fear begins to grip me. What if this is embarrassing? What if these joyful people see through my façade, see who I really am? An irresponsible degenerate in an uncontrollable depression? What if I can't do it right? Or even worse, what if I can? What if I do become joyful? What will life be without the familiar struggle, pain, fear, worry, self-hatred, anger, rage? What will be left of me? Who will I be? What will I do? It's just like me to worry—even about joy!

Okay, good. Now we're lost. This is a good thing. We're running late (as usual) and we're close, but lost. What a nice distraction from the panic I was feeling about a new, foreign experience. Being lost and late with no windshield washer fluid left on a drizzly day. Now, this is more like it! A nice comfy, familiar panic. I can live with this.

"Yes, ma, that must be it. I'm turning, see? My blinker is on."

Arrival. Six minutes late. I'm almost panting. The fear is loud now, filling my head with voices, scenes of humiliation and embarrassment.

Will I find the right building? How many people are in there? Will I find my sister? I'll tiptoe in, annoyed faces of consternation greeting me; I'll interrupt a solemn and peaceful ceremony, and they'll ignore me, everyone will ignore me. I'll be the only outsider. They'll all know it. At least I'm not the only one. My mother is here to take the heat too. But I'm really all alone. No one can feel my pain for me. I have to. I have to feel the pain. All alone.

Wait, there's Lois! Phew! She's outside. It hasn't started yet. Thank GOD! Now I'm safe, temporarily at least.

Walking into the room was less stressful than anticipated. The atmosphere was friendly, warm, somehow. Eye contact suddenly seemed easy and natural. Confidence grew as we sat in a large circle of about forty people. A twinge of nerves surfaced momentarily when I realized we would all have to introduce ourselves. But it subsided quickly as the intros began.

My unruly imagination had conjured the image of a roomful of Dalai Lama types connecting to each other on deeply spiritual levels, while I sat on the fringe, from the outside looking in—with the demeanor of one on the verge of a nervous breakdown. To my relief, everyone seemed rather *normal*—even me! I relaxed as people expressed fears and reservations. I admired their willingness to try anyway. My self-esteem improved as I noticed that this was exactly what I was doing: trying! I decided to admire myself. By the time it was my turn, I was anxious to introduce myself. I was proud to announce my decision to come and my reason for coming. My sister's promise.

I began to finally understand why she had dragged me here. Little did I know that this was just the beginning. As Judith began talking, my preconceived notion of her melted away. My self-demeaning imagination had envisioned an untouchable guru-type in long flowing robes speaking parables in angelic whispers.

Although Judith was none of those things, I had instantly recognized her as the one I had come to see. She had a natural warm glow and I immediately relaxed in familiarity—as if we were old friends. She was curiously humble, with a fun teaching style, and an absolutely joyful *(did I say that?)* smile! I felt more like a friend than a student. Part of me was amazed when I volunteered to go in front of the group and receive a breathing analysis!

As I walked toward her, I felt my face flush with a melange of excitement, embarrassment, fear and pride. In a dreamlike sequence, I realized I was drawing the eyes of everyone present to my 300-pound frame on purpose! Unheard of! A cacophony of voices inside my head struck up a chorus:

African American sistah: "You go, girlfriend!"

My morbidly-obese personal angel: "Ice cream, ice cream, you need Ding-Dongs and ice cream!"

Sleepy girl blinking eyes at the sun: "Is this the beginning of a courageous life?"

Giggly little girl, slightly mischievous: "I'm doing it! I'm really doing it!"

Some wise guy in a leather jacket: "Okay, so who you supposed to be? Sybil?"

I try not to look clumsy as I recline under Judith's kneeling posture. As I hear her voice in the distance, I'm sure that my efforts to appear relaxed are working. Then, suddenly, effort is unnecessary. Judith has placed her firm, warm hand on my upper chest. I immediately draw in a breath as I never have before. The voices go silent. She asks some specific questions about my childhood in a way that makes it easy to answer in front of all these strangers. She points out that my upper chest is not moving. Gently, she reminds me of some deeply buried truths about myself: I really don't have asthma; my heart center was virtually shut down long ago; and I hold on to ancient trauma that affects me still.

Big surprise, right? Yes and no. I've been depressed and anxious for so long that I'd forgotten there were causes. I mean, intellectually I knew, but I stifled that knowledge and chose to believe that I had no choice but to hide the truth about who I was. Shame was a constant in my life. Maybe the only constant besides pain.

The realizations began to reemerge while I was lying on that floor. Tears escaped as she asked me to repeat in my mind, "It's safe to open my heart… safe to express my love." The silent gasps (that would have been sobs if I didn't hold them back) came, and just as I began to choke them down she said, "It's safe to express my feelings."

I can't let myself sob in front of all these strangers! Cut that out, young lady! You know better. Get a Ding Dong. Ice cream, yeah!

Judith was saying something and then I heard voices in the room, which drew me back, and it was loud. They were all toning and Judith wanted me to take a deep breath and join them. At first I was afraid to be heard. *Children should be seen and not heard!!* But who would hear me in all this noise? Maybe it'll be fun!? I took a deep breath and went for it. *Aaaaaaaahhhhhhhh!* Another deep breath... *Aaaaaaaaaahhhhhhhhhh...*

I was amazed at how long I could hold the tone and then my next inhalation filled me up with more energy. I started to feel a little light-headed and tingly while pictures of my life story flew past my mind's eye at the speed of light, complete with emotion, in full living color. I watched as the group supported my verbal expression. Words were somehow unnecessary. I felt as if it was all just melting away. No need to talk it over and relive the pain. My body was vibrating, and Judith's comforting touch told me everything was okay.

"Good, good, Liz. It's safe to express my will," she was almost yelling so I could hear her. Yet she was loving me. I could feel her loving me. I felt safe. After making several long sounds, I continued to breathe with no effort at all. It was as if someone else was breathing me, yet it was deep and full.

"Now Liz is beginning to activate," Judith told the group. "How does that feel, Liz?" I could only shake my head and smile. There was so much going on inside me! I was feeling parts of my body that I didn't know existed. This all occurred in a matter of ten minutes. As I walked back to my seat, the only voices left were encouraging, peaceful, hopeful and giddy. Mmmmmmm, all this growth even before doing a session. But the best was yet to come.

Soon we were told to hook up with a student facilitator. I already liked Alison, the woman sitting next to me, so I chose her. As people made themselves comfortable around the room, I lay back, closed my eyes and gave myself over to whatever was coming. Though I was a bit self-conscious (especially with Mom just a few feet away), I didn't let the fear take over. Alison began by making sure I was comfortable, giving a short explanation of what to expect, and telling me that there was no way to make a mistake during a breathing session. *Whew! What a relief.*

The breath was more difficult at first than I had expected, but the toning was an unforeseen bonus. Toning, or sounding as some call it, seemed to be a remarkable technique to expel grief, anger, pain, anything negative. The room was filled with an incredible range of extraordinary sounds and emotions; it seemed as though all of our souls were intertwined in a celebration of life and love and joy. I seized upon this opportunity to really let loose. I mean, how often does anyone feel safe enough to scream out their pain? Ironically, expelling that pain was *joyful.*

I remember crying for a short time, but I was not *in* my pain; it was simply streaming out of me. Though it took me a while to get into the rhythm of the breathing pattern, I recognized its value and looked forward to mastering it. At the end of the half-hour session, I became conscious of an intense tingling sensation in my lips and the tips of my fingers. My mind was clear, my blood was pumping as if I had just run a mile and I felt like I was glowing. I was so *alive!* An instinctive and momentous decision was immediately thrust upon me by my higher self: this was my calling. *I must make this my life's work.*

Nothing had ever seemed so clear. Since I started working fourteen years ago at the age of eighteen, I had held over twenty jobs, engulfed in a perpetual search for a satisfying, enriching career, something with depth and meaning. Thankfully, years of frustration and struggle came to a halt that evening, as the answer came swiftly and easily.

That night as I lay down to sleep, I noted with pleasure that my mind was not whirring with anxiety—quite a stark contrast to every other night as far back as I could remember. There were some unnerving musings floating around, like "what if this isn't real? What if I wake up tomorrow and the effect has worn off?" But these thoughts were not intrusive. I easily allowed them to drift to the perimeter as I enjoyed the new quietude in my mind.

The next morning I was ready for another incredible experience. But, as expected, I had a renewed distrust in the reality of this "therapy." I felt great, but suspicion was still a diminutive voice, nagging from a deep chasm in my mind. In hindsight, I realize I had been allowing doubt a forum only to appease the sense that I was betraying my own historic belief system of: "Life is hard, it must be hard, and if it *isn't* hard you must be cheating."

But how could I cheat myself by being happy?

The ongoing argument in my head was off and running again: *You'll be cheating yourself out of the ability to communicate with those around you. How's that? Most of the people you know are miserable, right? You'll be betraying them. Remember how you felt about your sister's joy? Others will feel that way about you.*

True. But should I stay miserable just so I can retain miserable friends? Come to think of it, I don't really have any friends, just acquaintances. Well, they will be angry, or at least taken aback, right? Here you have no friends and you're willing to jeopardize the few relationships you do have. Wait a minute! Maybe if I change my life I'll make some new friends—did you ever think of that? Well, I— and if I become joyful others will want to follow—the way I did with my sister. What about that? Hmm? SILENCE. HA! I've stumped you. Now keep quiet while I enjoy my day.

Excitement sizzled in the air as I stepped into the large room for the breath clinic. Everyone seemed a lot more at ease this time and chatter was friendly and relaxed. I located a corner with my facilitator and she went to work making my space warm and cozy. We started with some Kundalini movement, which seemed to be a good catalyst to deep breathing, and then the session began. This time I was lying down with pillows supporting my upper torso and knees. I had brought my favorite comforter and used that to keep warm. Judith started us off with some inspired words and soothing music; talk about feeling pampered!

As we launched into a full hour of breathing, all of my previous doubts completely vanished. I felt a feeling I had never felt before, one of being *at home*. You see, all my life I have felt homesick, even when I was in my own home or visiting the house in which I grew up—I had a deep and unsettling sense that I didn't belong anywhere—that there was nowhere to call home. Having moved twelve times in the last fourteen years, I'd been searching all my life for the Place that would satisfy my discontent. Ironically, I found it in a conference room in a strange town with a stranger hovering over me. I realized then that home was not a geographical location, but a connection with God—the connection I'd always had, but had been ignoring since early childhood.

It's hard to put words to this whole experience, for none of this came to me on an intellectual level. In fact, none of my thoughts during the breath session were traditional thoughts that can be reported upon. Instead, the change occurred on a plane that I had never before visited.

A mellow yet vibrant energy was humming through my body, mind, and spirit, melting them into one perfectly seamless entity, no boundaries, no pain. Occasionally, I would become conscious of some cries emanating from my mother–agonizing screams, aching for that same bliss I was finding. My role as the family peacekeeper surfaced, momentarily, and I wanted to run and comfort her. I refrained, however, instantly realizing that she had to experience this on her own. These lapses back into old programming occurred for a fraction of a second and were quickly assimilated into the joy. *So this is what joy feels like?*

At the end of the session, my whole body was tingling, and I was in a state of ecstasy. I felt snuggly and warm as we all faced each other in a circle to share our stories. I was not surprised to find that many others were also describing their own incredible experiences as life-changing.

M*y goodness, what a difference a day makes!* My mother and I are in the car now, driving home. Bad drivers? What bad drivers? I'm driving home in a new world. Aaahhh. I am seeing in a different light and hearing on a different frequency. My mother's laments are less frequent, and those that do reach my ears have no negative effect whatsoever. I can't seem to wipe the almost imperceptible, very real smile off my face. I realize that it was my own self-condemnation that made Mom seem so condescending.

Upon arrival at my mess of a mobile home after an enjoyable four-hour ride with Mom, I look around the place and know it is just part of my past. I thank God for the opportunity to move onward.

In January, 1999, Liz, her ten-year-old son, Alex, and their dog, Buster, found a happy home with another single mom and her two children. She now finds pleasure in all the little things— cooking healthy meals, keeping her bedroom clean, losing weight, running a small marketing firm (www.thewriteagency.com) and a holistic health bartar network (fullcircleexchange.com). She is also certified as a Transformational Breathing Facilitator.

"Improper breathing
is a common cause
of ill health."

- Andrew Weil, M.D.

The Time Is Now

As many of us seek new avenues to health, longevity, peace, and prosperity, we usually overlook the most important thing we can do for ourselves: breathe. Most of us live our entire lives paying little or no attention to how we breathe. We have no clue as to the importance of proper breathing and how deeply it affects the quality of our lives.

In this complex modern world, it has become more crucial than ever to breathe effectively. Time seems to rule our lives; many of us are continually rushing. Air quality is often poor. Crowded cities and chaotic schedules give us plenty of fuel for chronic states of stress. Never has human breathing been so restricted; for many, breathing capacity is all but completely shut down.

In our unconscious terror of being alone to fend for ourselves against a perceived "big bad world," we huff and puff at each other and frequently do everything in our power to prevent the flow of feelings. When faced with emotions we don't want to feel, we stifle the flow of breath and, therefore, the flow of Life Force energy.

Very few people have understood the incredible healing and creative power that can be claimed by learning to expand and control our own breath. This is not so surprising, when we consider that healthy breathing is not taught anywhere in our educational system. The complete science of effective breathing is not even addressed in modern yoga classes. Nor is it adequately addressed in the training of athletes, dancers, singers, health care workers, or other professions in which oxygen supply is crucial. Although all of these practices do utilize various forms of conscious breathing, the science of creating open, unrestricted breathing is not truly known or shared as an integral part of any of these activities.

Much of the information in this book seems new to modern civilization; however, it is actually a revival of ancient knowledge. We have been redirected to it at this time because of the great need to effect positive change in our world. Personal healing and transformation through the breath is a gift that humanity has been given to help us save ourselves at a time of possible self-destruction. We are entering an era of looming prophecies and it has been made quite clear that how we respond to current challenges will determine the earthly outcome. There is strong evidence that our modern way of life could change drastically, due to lack of foresight in our own technological advances.

Conscious breathing allows us to respond calmly and sensibly in the face of potential challenges. Through breathing, we gain the ability to respond creatively to anything that may arise in our lives and our world without the need for either denial or panic.

In Dr. Norma J. Milanovich's popular book, *We, The Arcturians; A True Experience*, full conscious breathing is emphasized as "the key to mastering the electronic force of the universe and the power to manifest the fifth dimension."

This extraordinary statement is consistent with the seemingly miraculous results many people achieve from Transformational Breathing. While training people to breathe better, I have witnessed them overcome life-threatening diseases, addictions, and psychiatric disorders.

I no longer consider these experiences miracles. I have come to realize they are a natural result of returning to the essence of being. Our breathing can take us there.

The very first thing we do in Transformational Breathing is teach people how to breathe fully and deeply. We help them to discover and then retrain their own restricted patterns of breathing. Practiced in dedicated hour-long sessions, Transformational Breathing is a self-responsible healing method that employs a high-vibrational energy, created by the breath, to clear the low-vibrational charge of disease and restricted cellular memory.

Primarily created by a specific circular breathing pattern, this high-vibrational state allows for deep resolution of what Dr. Wayne Dyer calls our *erroneous zones* (toxic errors in thinking). The breath causes full integration of body, feelings, mind, and spirit.

This highly developed form of breath therapy allows us to tap into unlimited energy and discover who we are at the deepest levels. Eventually, the same full, open, and connected breathing pattern practiced in the breath sessions starts to carry over into everyday living. After just a few sessions with a breath coach / facilitator, we begin maximizing oxygen intake and increasing our energy and vitality.

Soon we sense a new freedom to experience and express the natural states of joy, unconditional love, and peaceful power that are always abundantly available to each of us regardless of external events. We can even gain the unshakable faith needed to hold fast to the reality of love's power in the face of the darkest storm.

Some of us have a hard time committing to doing something good for ourselves, considering it a sign of weakness or selfishness. In truth, however, doing good for ourselves is really an act of giving, because it provides us with the awareness and energy to give a great deal more than we otherwise could! Furthermore, when we move and act from a sense of inner peace and power, we help others to respond in kind. This will begin to spread exponentially and outer peace will soon prevail as well. We all win.

I invite you to join us as we move toward a world of peace. This book can help us upgrade our own state of mind and contribute to a larger pool of awareness that affects all minds. This principle is well illustrated by the "hundredth monkey" phenomenon, based on a study of animal behavior that was reported by the late Ken Keyes, Jr., in his ground-breaking book, *The Hundredth Monkey*.

In brief summary, monkeys living on an isolated island were taught by humans to wash potatoes before eating them—a behavior that had never been observed in simian society. Shortly thereafter, this same behavior was observed for the first time in numerous locations across the world. The island-bound monkeys had no way of directly teaching other monkeys to wash potatoes. It seems there is a kind of "information superhighway," more often referred to as a "universal mind," that connects all minds.

Larry Dossey, M.D., author of numerous works on spirituality, healing, and the power of prayer, calls it the "non-local mind." When we pray with faith or declare affirmative statements, we consciously redirect the flow of our own thoughts. This, in turn, affects the universal mind and thus all individual minds.

In his book, *I'll See It When I Believe It*, Herbert Benson, M.D., also offers compelling evidence that we actively affect our universe. He cites more than sixty clinical studies demonstrating that prayer does work; that a part of us reaches out beyond time and space and communicates with all of us. This is how we create our experiences: we invite into our lives whatever we believe in. We see it when we believe it.

Transformational Breathing gives us greater access to the universal mind, so that we may gain clear insight and take appropriate and timely action, instead of putting things off or panicking in the face of change. We can also choose to affect the universal mind in positive ways. By embracing and appreciating it, we find ultimate safety in ourselves because we learn how to *create* what we want instead of trying to *get* what we want.

Soon we find ourselves preparing for exciting adventures in life instead of hiding from ugly thoughts of doom and gloom. With a change of perspective and the energy to respond fully, problems become opportunities, and the idea of denying or resisting circumstances is revealed as unnecessary self-sabotage.

Breathing freely releases the mind from the bondage of negative thoughts, so you can choose exactly when and where to focus time and attention for maximum results. It also brings us to a place of knowing what we can truly achieve for the good of all concerned. Ultimately, Transformational Breathing allows us to refocus our attention on the awesome power of our most basic connection with Life Force.

My sincerest wish is that in your mind the word *breathe* will soon become as sweet as the sound of children laughing, and that you will unleash that same playful joy from within your own heart— joy that longs to sing out loud and clear.

Creating Vibrant Health

Working with thousands of people in groups and private sessions, I have found that nearly eighty percent of Americans suffer from severely restricted breathing patterns. On average, they are only taking in twenty to thirty percent of their actual lung capacity. With so many of us starving our cells for oxygen, is it any wonder there is an epidemic of people feeling tired all the time? We are unknowingly depriving ourselves of the most vital energy for optimal health.

Shallow breathing has been linked to an astonishing number of physical and emotional disorders as well as catastrophic diseases. In these pages, you will get a glimpse at the lives of many people whose health has been dramatically restored once they chose to practice healthy breathing.

Let's be clear about this: I have never cured or healed anyone—except myself. And even if I could legally make such a claim, I would never do so. I have come to know that all healing is *self*-healing. Whenever we attempt to shift responsibility for our own health onto someone else, like a breath coach or, for that matter, a doctor, we effectively relinquish our innate power to heal. It is worth stating again: Transformational Breathing is a *self-responsible* healing method. Facilitators provide guidance and support, but only you can breathe for you. Your healing and transformation are entirely in your own hands.

Effective breathing is your most important tool for creating physical, mental, and spiritual well-being. In a world whose economy is driven by high-tech solutions, how could this be so?

1. Oxygen is the most essential natural resource required by our cells. It has been said that we can go without food for up to forty days and without water for three days. Yet we can die after just a few minutes of not breathing. From a purely physical viewpoint, breath equals life.

2. Approximately seventy-five percent of our body's blood circulation is located in the mid- and lower torso. When we breathe deeply, we directly nourish these blood vessels with essential oxygen. When we breathe shallowly, we *deprive* the body of its most-needed life-giving nutrient.

3. Breathing stimulates the electrochemical processes of every cell in our bodies: skin, organs, muscles, bones, blood, etc. The breath is their primary delivery system for food and electrical charge (energy).

4. Deep diaphragmatic breathing tones and massages the heart, liver and *all* other internal organs and muscles including the brain and reproductive organs! An ingenious system of eight diaphragms, connecting the body from head to foot, stimulates every part of the body when the abdominal diaphragm expands and contracts. (See Appendix B for more details.)

5. Inhaling oxygen strengthens the immune system, while exhaling expels toxins. Shallow breathers literally poison themselves, because most toxins are released through the breath. When we don't breathe sufficiently, toxins remain in the body, running through the entire elimination system *again*, and back into circulation.

6. Breathing also plays an important role in determining mental and emotional states which, if allowed to deteriorate, can contribute to psychological stress and disease.

7. Mental acuity, the ability to learn and assimilate information, focus, concentrate, and remember, are all greatly affected by the quality of breathing, since the brain requires a great deal of oxygen to function.

Considering the obvious importance of breathing the way nature intended, why is it that so many of us breathe inadequately?

It's a matter of conditioning and training. Breathing is the one autonomic, involuntary metabolic process that can become voluntary the moment we make a conscious *choice* to take a breath. Since the body continues to breathe on its own when we choose to ignore it, it is no surprise that many of us take our breathing for granted.

In-depth studies of modern-day yogis, such as Swami Rama (co-author, *Science of Breath*), have proven to scientists that it is also quite possible to control heartbeat, metabolism and other involuntary bodily functions. Not surprisingly, such skills typically require many years of discipline and training in *conscious breathing* techniques. The breath is the gateway to the subconscious mind – the place where *automatic* functions, patterns and habits are stored and may be accessed.

Although our self-mastery goals may not be the same as a yogi's, many important benefits are immediately available through conscious breathing. The moment we choose to take the reins of our breathing, we can alter our restricted breathing patterns and begin to live in a more positive state of mind – and body. We can make this choice *at any time*, regardless of circumstances around us. When we don't take advantage of our ability to do so, we tend to be at the mercy of our subconscious, automatic reactions.

Some people may even feel aggravated by the very idea that we have a *choice* in how we experience life. After years of conditioning to the contrary, it has become a common misperception that unpleasant feelings are the result of being a victim of circumstance.

Right now is a perfect opportunity to demonstrate this innate ability to yourself, and have some fun at the same time. Here's a little appetizer of what conscious breathing can do for you.

Sit or lie down comfortably; then take a moment to get quiet. Notice how you are feeling in this moment.

Place your hands on your belly, open your mouth wide, relax your jaw, and take the biggest breath you can imagine. Breathe through your mouth only, bringing the air all the way down into your belly. Feel those abdominal muscles working, even if you must lean back and slouch down a little, and consciously push the belly out against your hands while inhaling. Then feel the inhalation rise up into your chest.

At the top of the inhalation, when you feel full to the brim and no more air will fit in, just let it fall back out in a big relaxing, voiceless sigh. Then without pausing, immediately inhale again, exactly as before.

Meanwhile, smile in your mind (your mouth is busy receiving) and think about how grateful your cells are for this sudden attention. Take in self-appreciation for what you are doing. Take fifteen more breaths without pausing between inhaling and exhaling.

Ready? Set? Go.

I'll wait, happily.

Okay, are you feeling any different?

You have just experienced a taste of your ability to alter your experience. This breath is called the Breath to Joy, and I recommend that my students practice 100 Breaths to Joy every day. It is a wonderful way to start opening up your breathing and will also make longer sessions easier. (See the coupon at the back of the book to receive the free tape, *100 Breaths to Joy*. My students find this tape really helps them focus and continue to progress between sessions.)

I'm going to ask you to make a pact with yourself. Promise that you will take three deep, connected breaths any time you feel tense or catch yourself not breathing. And I suggest doing this fifteen-breath exercise before starting each new chapter. In so doing, you will be well on your way to experiencing some of the glorious benefits of deep Transformational Breathing.

When left to the unconscious realm, breathing can become increasingly shallow and restricted. One reason for this is that we have been conditioned to hold our breath under stressful circumstances. As children, most of us were repeatedly told to stop crying when we were hurt or upset, or quiet down when we were excited and happy. This is how spirit is broken. We learned that, in order to be accepted, we had to suppress feelings unacceptable to others. The only way to stifle feelings is by holding our breath.

While holding the breath may ease the intensity of our feelings in the moment, it does not make them go away. It simply pushes them to a subconscious level, where we then express them in other, unexpected (perhaps even automatic) ways. Keeping repressed emotions and trauma from resurfacing requires tremendous determination and energy—all unconscious, of course. Our continued shallow and restricted breathing patterns become habitual, costing us still more energy and creating chronic tension in our bodies.

Another primary cause of closed and restricted breathing patterns has to do with our very first breath. At the moment of birth, each of us established the basic foundation of our relationship to our bodies and to breathing itself. For most of us it was a traumatic first impression. The majority of us were born in a hospital, where birth is considered a medical emergency.

For reasons that have nothing to do with the infant's needs, the traditional practice is to cut the umbilical cord immediately after birth, cutting off our oxygen supply abruptly and throwing us into extreme stress in the middle of a huge transition. Our tiny, fluid-filled lungs had to open very quickly. Being forced into taking our very first breath unexpectedly and in a state of panic, induced the sensations of suffocation and abandonment. We were rushed into accepting respiration according to someone else's time schedule. (See Joseph Chilton Pearce's *The Magical Child* for a full description of this type of birth and its ramifications.)

Surely nature intended this major transition to be a more gradual, gentle, joyful experience. Most of us, however, experienced searing pain with this first premature breath and adopted the belief that it is painful to breathe. From that moment forward, many of us began to resist breathing because of the learned subconscious belief that breathing hurts. It did hurt, in more ways than one.

Many of us still struggle frantically to regain an internal sense of dignity and control that was lost in the midst of a birthing process that disregarded our most basic natural needs. The message was loud and clear: Breathe on our terms, or die. It was literally a matter of life and death.

Our breathing becomes restricted from the very first breath and then continues to build upon this foundation. As an integral part of socialization, ongoing training in holding back our feelings and our breath has become deeply rooted in our entire being.

If we are not breathing fully, we suffer. Our lives remain marginal at best. The good news is that our entire being—body, mind and spirit—can be transformed by permanently changing the way we breathe.

Anatomy of a Breathing Session

Early in my own self-healing journey, I was surprised to find that each breathing session was completely new and different from any of my prior experiences. Even more surprising is the fact that after twenty years of facilitating both my own and others' breathing sessions, it still holds true. Aside from some clear and unmistakable signs and cycles that guide the facilitator in assisting the process, each session is as unique as the individual breathing in that very moment of time.

What unfolds during any given session depends primarily upon the intention of the person breathing and what is most needed for their highest good at the time. Although there is no such thing as a typical Transformational Breathing session, in this chapter we'll discuss procedures and components that are common to most sessions and give you a pretty good idea of what to expect your first time.

A session usually lasts about an hour and a half, beginning with a short interview. You may be asked to share some pertinent personal information and health history so that the facilitator can have an idea of potential issues that might emerge. It will also be helpful to talk briefly about your perceptions and feelings regarding your present-day circumstances.

The information shared is not as important as the rapport established between you and your coach. The interview allows you both to relax and get acquainted with each other, and hopefully establishes a sense of comfort and trust between you. This is a time to voice any questions and concerns you may have. And most importantly, it is a time for you to set out your intention for this breathing session. The key question is, "What do you want more of in your life?"

Your facilitator, or coach, will give you an explanation and demonstration of the full, connected breath. She will then do an analysis of your breathing. By discovering the specific ways in which your breathing is shut down, your coach can develop a plan for the best way to help you repattern old dysfunctional breathing habits.

There will be a comfortable place for you to lie down with plenty of pillows and blankets. There may be some music playing, specifically chosen to enhance your experience. Once you are as comfortable and relaxed as possible, your coach will guide you into achieving and maintaining the full, connected breathing pattern. This may include verbal guidance, affirmations, repositioning the body, and gentle or firm touch to the blocked areas of the body.

The value of affirmations is well known by self-help leaders and enthusiasts. Louise Hay, for example, bestselling author of *You Can Heal Your Life*, has developed a whole program for health and wellness based primarily upon the use of affirmations. These self-liberating statements of fundamental truths displace negative input with positive input. While the circular breathing is holding open the door to the subconscious mind, they are more readily accepted and the results are faster and more efficient.

Invocations, spoken aloud, serve to establish the highest purpose for the session. The coach may call upon your Higher Self, God, Higher Power, Holy Spirit, Angels, or Spirit Guides to bring forth your highest good from the perspective of Divine Intelligence. The words used will vary somewhat among facilitators, and are not as important as the intention of inviting assistance. Feel free to indicate your own preference if you have one.

Often the easiest way to get started is to simply breathe along with your facilitator as she models the ideal breath. Such a breath is like a wave rising and falling in a smooth, uninterrupted motion. We refer to it as circular because there is no pausing or holding the breath between inhaling and exhaling. It sometimes helps to envision your breath as a circle of light and focus on that.

The ideal inhalation is long and full-bodied, and the exhalation is quick and relaxed. No need to push the river. Make no effort whatsoever to force the breath out of your lungs, nor to draw your stomach back toward the spine. By asking your body to relax each time you exhale, you unwind stored tension in the body, creating a deeper sense of safety, which further supports your process.

We breathe through the mouth during the initial sessions to allow the greatest volume of air to pass through. The nose is too narrow a passageway to maximize the breath as required, and is prone to clogging, particularly during emotional periods. Oral breathing also opens the lower energy centers, frequently called *chakras* (a Sanskrit word meaning "wheels").

Although many yogis prefer breathing through the nose (or a combination of nose and mouth breathing for some exercises), we find that nose breathing primarily activates the upper chakras. Doing this before balancing and unblocking lower ones can be counterproductive, because the increased energy in the upper chakras would merely strengthen the block of denied negativity in the lower chakras.

We do not alternate between nose and mouth breathing, as this interrupts the energy circuit crucial for the process to work.

As the session proceeds, you will find yourself breathing in a way you have probably never experienced before. It may feel foreign and uncomfortable at first, but this will soon pass. You will be bringing a great deal of oxygen into your body, which will stimulate many new sensations and feelings.

One of the first and most common sensations you may feel is tingling throughout the body. This is a sign of energy moving, and of existing energy frequencies being raised to a higher rate of vibration. Feeling light-headed is not unusual, although many people confuse it with dizziness. When examined more closely, you will probably realize that you are not really dizzy. You are simply unaccustomed to the feeling of lightness that comes with increased oxygen to the brain.

Another thing you may experience is a sensation of being hot or cold. This is one possible reaction to toxins moving out of your system. A great variety of other powerful sensations, emotions, memories, and beliefs may come into your awareness. They tend to intensify and then dissolve as you breathe through them.

Initially, you may feel that it is difficult to breathe in this full, connected rhythm. Remember, you are changing lifelong dysfunctional habits. There is really nothing difficult about this way of breathing; it only seems so because of associations that bind our minds to old lingering beliefs. Like anything else we try for the first time, Transformational Breathing may take a little practice.

Your coach will be giving you positive affirmations to support your subconscious mind in letting go of those old self-limiting beliefs. You may find it helpful to silently repeat these affirming statements, but it is not necessary to do so. These very simple fundamental statements are effective at displacing the self-limiting beliefs that are linked with certain restricted breath patterns. They may stir up feelings, too, and this is helpful. Your job is simply to notice and accept what comes up while continuing to breathe without pausing.

Another helpful technique is called *toning*. At various times in the session, your coach will ask you to make as full a sound as possible, beginning after you inhale and continuing through the entire exhalation. She may join you in order to relieve any self-conscious tendencies, but it is not necessary to match her pitch or timing. In fact, it is important not to try to control the sound in any way. Simply relax your throat as much as possible and make the fullest, biggest sound that will come out. As soon as you need more air, inhale without pausing and make another tone. Toning is most helpful in sets of three or more.

Although your coach will suggest toning at times, feel free to initiate it yourself whenever you think it may be useful. Toning can be used to help initiate activation (the experience of the breath breathing *us*) or moderate energy flow if anything seems overwhelming. Toning also provides an effective alternative to crying, as it moves the energy through faster and more readily.

Sound is a very high-frequency expression of pure energy. If you let your body make the sound it wants to make, it will always make the right sound for whatever healing is required. If the sound is not pleasant to the ear, the best thing is to continue toning until it shifts to a harmonic tone. You will feel the vibration in parts of your body where healing is taking place.

During much of the session, your facilitator may be applying touch. This is required for several reasons. Firm touch is used to relax respiratory muscles and help direct the breath into blocked areas. Applying firm pressure to the abdominal area, for example, opens that area. Pressure on the solar plexus muscle allows breath to be drawn into the upper chest, and we relax more fully as we exhale.

Touch is also used to discover, trigger, and release the blocked energies of repressed emotions. Using a technique called body mapping, facilitators learn the correlations between specific points of tension in the body and corresponding emotional blockages. Applying pressure to these points, while giving appropriate affirmations, activates cellular memory and emotion and encourages the breather to safely express the emotion.

And finally, touch is an important way to provide gentle, nurturing support, aimed at enhancing your ability to relax into a new experience of safety throughout the session. Naturally, it is always important to let your coach know if a touch is distracting or interfering with your experience, or if there is something that would make your session more effective for you. It is okay—and important—to ask for what you want.

At some point during the session, usually within the first fifteen minutes, you will "activate," and the breathing will suddenly seem very easy. You might feel like the breath is breathing you. From that point on, you will exert very little to no effort, yet the breath will keep on going, even more strongly than when you were really working at it.

Activation is mysterious, magical, and well worth whatever effort it takes to get there. During this stage is when deep healing and transformation take place. It can last thirty to forty minutes or more. Because you have shifted into deeper states of consciousness while activated, it may seem like just a few minutes.

It is quite amazing to observe the flow and movement of the breath while one is activated. The breath appears to take on an intelligence of its own, knowing exactly where to go and what to do. And why wouldn't it? It is, in great part, Life Force energy—the primal, creative intelligence of the Universe—which we are welcoming into our being. I believe that this mysterious state of activation opens us to the miraculous benefits of Transformational Breathing.

While activated, you will go through cycles of "integration," experienced as changing energy patterns or as distinct changes in your physical and emotional feelings. For example, as you are breathing, you may begin to notice some tension in the back of your neck and some feelings of anger. If you continue to focus on and breathe into that area, allowing yourself to fully embrace those feelings, you will probably notice that the sensations are really just energy. And next you will notice that, as you continue to breathe into them, they change. The tension may melt slowly away, or completely release in an instant.

One client described this experience: "The tension in my arms and legs was so strong it began to hurt. But I remembered what my coach told me – this was old stuff integrating. I smiled and toned and kicked and punched as she suggested. Suddenly the pain turned into pulsing waves of pleasure. My body and mind felt melded into liquid gold. The elation was like nothing I'd ever experienced."

Anger often transforms into feelings such as love or joy. Grief and sorrow may be replaced by peace or joyful laughter. Such shifts are a clear indication that the original pattern has been permanently transformed. The key to getting to the other side is opening to the process and, instead of resisting or judging them, embracing the sensations in your body.

Most importantly, keep breathing! Once feelings are stimulated, it is important to continue the circular breathing until you reach the other side of them. Once they have integrated, unpleasant feelings give way to very pleasant ones. I have observed breathers passing through as many as twenty integration cycles in a single session, while in other, equally powerful, sessions, only a couple of cycles occurred.

The number of these integration cycles varies with each session, depending upon the patterns coming up and how willingly we surrender to them. Surrender means opening up and allowing ourselves to experience the energy, feelings, and breath. We embrace them, rather than judging, controlling, or resisting them.

It is important to realize that conscious memories are not required for integration of repressed trauma to occur. Emotions often arise with no conscious memory of where they originated. In fact, sometimes integration is experienced as pure physical sensation, with no associated memories or emotions. For example, we may experience tightness and tingling in the jaw and face and a changing stream of many other sensations during a breathing session. Although we may not experience emotions or memories along with the physical shifts, it is highly probable that we are integrating repressed anger commonly stored and held back in the jaw.

During the activation phase, it is very important to trust this intelligence and surrender to the flow of energies moving within us. It is important not only to let ourselves feel whatever arises, but to freely express it as well. Expression can take many forms such as coughing, toning, laughing, crying, shouting, and moving. Relax. Know this is all perfectly healthy and absolutely acceptable.

Your facilitator will be well prepared and unconditionally supportive. We facilitators have been through it all ourselves and with many others. Our intention is to encourage the expression and integration of emotions and feelings as they surface. The last thing we want to do in a breath session is repress them further!

As a breather, if you resist and hold back, you may feel some discomfort and perhaps even stop the integration process altogether. As you surrender and accept the feelings, you may begin to feel as if you are riding on waves of breath. Either way, your coach will be right there with you to witness and revel in your progress. This is a joyful experience for both of you.

The best possible results come with the deliberate decision to say yes to whatever occurs, without judging yourself as doing it wrong. Remember that no matter how you respond or react to your experience, you are breathing in much more oxygen than you normally do, and this is good for your body, mind, and spirit. You cannot lose! If you do experience self-judgment, notice it and realize that this is simply another life and breath pattern that will be healed—if not in this breath session, then in a later one.

At some point during the session, your breathing will start to settle down. Although it will still be full, open, and connected, it will become gentler and not so intense. Your coach will say another invocation asking for a clear sign of connection with the Higher Self. After he senses a shift in your state of mind, he will ask that you open to whatever gifts you are ready to receive for your greatest good at this time. He will then remind you to breathe in your intention for the session.

As you welcome the oxygen into your body, consciously welcome your intention into your life. You may find that during the session your focus has shifted and altered your original intention. This is perfectly normal and part of the transformational process. Breathing in your intention allows you to consciously participate in the co-creation of your desired good. You may actually feel this phenomenon take place as you free your imagination and envision every cell of your body receiving the breath and your intention.

In the final phase of the breathing session, your awareness opens to higher levels of consciousness. This is accomplished through conscious invocation and through the energetic vacuum that was created through the breathing. You will probably find yourself in an extremely relaxed and deeply meditative state in which you can open to receiving guidance from the higher dimensional aspects of self. You may even have a mystical experience or receive a vision or clear guidance.

Some people experience their true self for the first time–a self who was always there, of course, but mostly overshadowed by layers of repressed negativity and fear. This awareness is truly one of the most amazing aspects of Transformational Breathing.

It is important to let go of comparisons and expectations. Trusting that each breathing session is perfect for what we most need at the time actually accelerates the perfect resolution of whatever emerges. This truth is not only reflected in our feelings of clarity, lightness, and joy immediately following the session, but particularly in the outer changes that manifest in our lives from that time forward.

Breath Analysis:
Mapping the Subconscious

Your current breathing patterns provide a kind of map to your personality. By illustrating both conscious and unconscious behavior patterns, your breathing presents literal and metaphorical information about how you see yourself and how you perceive and respond to life. To the trained eye, in fact, what you do with your breath clearly reflects what you do with the Life Force itself.

The art and science of understanding and revealing the direct relationship between your breathing and your life experience is called *breath analysis.* In addition to telling us how you're treating yourself and your life, breath analysis also provides the guidelines necessary to retrain your breathing.

In a day and age when life can seem so complex and every problem or symptom known to man is answered with an expensive new patented drug, this approach may seem too simple to be valid. After a few breathing sessions, however, it all begins to make perfect sense as you discover a much more pleasant and self-responsible attitude toward life in general.

Limiting beliefs and their resulting self-sabotaging behaviors can best be cleared by changing your breathing patterns. We must first determine what these patterns are, however, in order to take proper corrective measures. If we consider the way we breathe as a metaphor for how we live our lives, it becomes obvious that as we restrict our flow of breath we likewise impede the natural flow of our lives. By focusing intention on redirecting our breath, we begin to experience an intentional relationship with the Life Force, which is our creative power. Once we revive this creative flow, we begin to choose breath instead of drugs, and love and joy instead of fear and pain.

Breath analysis is the first step to engaging such a dynamic upswing in your life. By observing closely the sometimes-subtle movements of your body as you breathe, the facilitator can begin to assist you in making corrections and programming them into the involuntary breath mechanism for lasting change.

There are two primary considerations: First, which areas of the respiratory system are being utilized? Second, how much air are you taking in and letting out? There are also several important factors involving the flow of the breath: we observe where the breath goes first, where it pauses or gets blocked, and how much time is spent inhaling compared to exhaling. Each of these factors gives us clues about physical condition as well as behavioral and emotional tendencies.

To determine which areas of the respiratory system are being utilized, we begin by observing the lower abdomen. Does it rise and fall with each breath? Is the breath flowing into the pelvic area? Remember that approximately seventy-five percent of our blood circulates in the mid- and lower torso, so full, deep breaths are crucial to good health. When we store tension from unacknowledged feelings in various parts of our body, we also restrict our breathing; the diaphragm is not engaged, and we waste the power of our most important respiratory muscle. (Later we'll discuss the far-reaching effects of using the diaphragm.) Restricted, tense, or shallow breathing can show a fear response, while deep belly breathing relaxes us and produces pleasure-giving endorphins. To attain optimal breathing, we must begin by rebuilding this deep abdominal foundation.

Energetically speaking, the abdomen is the seat of the subconscious, which is why strong belly-breathing permits access to and clearing of the subconscious mind. Not surprisingly, about one-third of the people I have facilitated are not initially breathing into this area at all, which indicates they may strongly resist being here in a body. We refer to this as the "unconscious death urge." If not retrained to breathe abdominally, these people tend to continue with self-destructive behavior and often develop problems in the lower back, digestive system, and/or regenerative organs.

The personal will also resides in the belly. Abdominal breathers, therefore, are strong-willed, creative people. They are also very grounded and in tune with their bodies. Conversely, those who do not breathe into the lower abdomen usually have less personal will and are more likely to be taken advantage of or dominated. They also tend to hold on to self-judgment and guilt. People with no breath or shallow breath in their bellies often feel spacey and unfocused. The tendency to be ungrounded is common, since they are not fully connected with the body. One common example of this, in women, is not being aware of physical sensations that indicate onset of the menstrual period. Strong belly-breathers, on the other hand, can often feel even the subtlest of physical sensations, such as ovulation or the conception of a child.

To achieve deep belly breathing (also known as strong diaphragmatic breathing), consciously focus on pulling the breath into the lower abdomen while affirming: "It is safe to be in my body. I am completely safe. I forgive myself completely." Sometimes facilitators place ten-pound sacks of sand, called belly bags, on the breather's lower abdomen. This pressure instigates counter-pressure and is very effective for retraining the associated muscles to flex and release.

As this area opens up, new feelings of safety and self-acceptance start replacing shame and self-judgment in the subconscious mind. This gives the body-mind long-overdue permission to allow Life Force to flow freely into previously restricted areas. Creativity once blocked is now liberated, leading to more energy, a more grounded presence, and a good sense of self-direction.

Next we look at the solar plexus and diaphragmatic area, located in the middle of the respiratory system. Lack of breath in the midsection represents a separation between heart and will. In other words, blocked breathing in this area reveals the belief that following our heart will keep us from doing what we need to do. If you have this pattern, you may describe yourself as constantly feeling pulled in two directions, as if you are leading two separate lives. You may suffer from inordinate fear, worry or possibly panic attacks.

To open this area, manual pressure is placed on the solar plexus to tap off some of the tension while affirming, "My heart and will are one. It is safe to follow my heart." The combination of physical and emotional stimulation invites the muscles to release and draw breath into this area, resulting in the integration of heart and will. Once both the lower and mid-abdominal areas open, the breather can experience full-belly, diaphragmatic breathing.

We next look for movement in the upper torso. Lack of breathing in the sternum area represents a closed heart center and the repression of love. At some time in the past, a conscious or unconscious decision was made to shut down the feelings or heart of the person's experience. Often this is an early-childhood reaction to very strong-willed parents. Children shut down in order to protect themselves emotionally and maintain their personal will in order to survive in a strong-willed environment.

If our chest appears puffed out and rigid, as if not emptying upon exhaling, it indicates that we are holding on to old grief and anger. When we do this, we cannot freely receive or express love. Toning and raising the upper torso with pillows are two ways to support redirecting the breath into the upper respiratory system. Breathing fully and freely into the chest while affirming "It is safe to give and receive love; it is safe to express my feelings," facilitates the unblocking and transforming of repressed, painful feelings. This in turn allows the flow of love to expand in and out, to and from us.

The uppermost chest area (above the heart) and throat are where the expression or repression of Higher Will occurs. Often the will to express our true mission in this life gets thwarted and forgotten, especially if we grew up in an environment where expressing our personal will was not permitted. The personal will, seated in the lower abdomen, is the drive to fulfill our human needs and desires (for example, comfort, food, and shelter). Higher Will goes beyond the personal will. It is the will of Spirit and refers to our higher purpose for being here.

If the upper chest area is not moving visibly during a breath, or the throat is constricted, chances are we feel a lack of empowerment and direction. We may be confused as to the meaning of life and why we are really here. If the upper respiratory area is almost *completely* closed down, we likely have little or no clarity about the purpose for our life, and have shut down our expression of love as well.

By focusing on really filling up that area as we inhale, while repeating affirmations such as, "It is safe to express my will. My will and God's will are one," we transform repressed emotions by allowing ourselves to experience them. Expressions of Higher Will begin to emerge, and we reawaken to the passion for life and openness to love that we had as children.

When a breathing analysis reveals full movement in all areas of the respiratory system, particularly while maintaining the connected breath pattern, we are very open, trusting, and comfortable with the flow of life. We have an accepting, easygoing relationship with life. We are "in the flow."

The order of the flow of breath is another revealing indicator. Ideally, the breath flows as follows: first into the lower abdomen, then the middle respiratory area, upper chest, and throat area. If the breath starts in the upper respiratory area, it is difficult, if not impossible, to make its way downward. In this case, the lower sections typically remain closed.

If the breath starts in the middle, we have a superachiever or perhaps a perfectionist personality. We probably have trouble delegating and believe we have to do it all ourselves or it won't get done—at least not to our standards! Pressing on the solar plexus, while inhaling, channels breath into the lower abdomen. Affirmations such as "It is safe to let go. I allow myself to be helped and supported. I let go and let God," are particularly useful in transforming the trust issues underlying this breathing pattern.

Next we look at how much air volume is being taken in. The in-breath illustrates our relationship to the positive flow of life, the inflow of abundance and good. How much of what we want are we actually willing to receive? If we filter our intake of air by partially closing our lips, breathing through clenched teeth, or blocking the throat with our tongue, we (at least partially) block the abundant flow of life energy available to us. We probably feel that we never have enough, or perhaps *any*, of what we want in our lives.

Jack is a sixty-five-year-old man who always claimed his children and grandchildren took priority in his life. However, he seldom put any energy into developing adult relationships with his four grown children and their children. He complained of the lack of closeness, but made few attempts to be close, emotionally or physically, never showing much interest in their lives, even when they got together for holidays. Instead, he was withdrawn and distant, and virtually ignored his grandchildren. Still, he complained that nobody came to visit him and continued to wonder why his life was so devoid of the loving relationships he desired.

Jack's breath analysis revealed that he was filtering his in-breath—exactly what one would expect from someone blocking his own flow of abundance. His breathing also showed he was repressing his ability to experience the flow of intimacy and expression in relationships. Jack's jaw was clenched so tight, in fact, that the breath whistled as it entered and departed. For most of his first breathing session, it would have required a sledgehammer to loosen up his jaw, and his throat muscles quivered quite visibly with tension. Toning helped release the tension, and his jaw finally dropped open toward the end. He was finally receiving instead of struggling to get what he wanted.

After that first breath session, one of his daughters reported that for the first time in years, she received a real hug from her dad. "He actually held me in his arms instead of patting my back and then pushing me away." Jack reported feeling more relaxed and connected with his children as well.

A diabetic, Jack also reported that his sugar count had been much easier to maintain afterward, indicating that he is not resisting the "sweets" of life as much as he once did. Although this analysis may sound esoteric, it is easily understood on a very physical level. Remember the simple fact that oxygen is the most fundamental unit of fuel our body requires in order to function. Whether we realize it or not, everything we do in order to take care of ourselves—eating, exercising, breathing, drinking water, taking vitamins and herbs—supplies our body with oxygen. Oxygen cleanses the cells and allows them to create energy. If we don't have any energy (sound familiar?), how can we possibly be available to experience what we want—even if it is sitting right in front of us? Without sufficient oxygen and energy, the body becomes sick. Illness further keeps us from what we want, and the proverbial snowball keeps on rolling down the hill faster and faster.

Yet even sick people can be coached to breathe better and start bringing in more oxygen. When they do so, more of what they consider "good" will come into their lives, too. It is logical, then, that a high-volume inhalation signifies an ability to accept goodness in one's life. It also gives them more energy to respond to what they consider good.

Conversely, a very shallow inhale indicates feelings of unworthiness and a lack of self-acceptance. This negative self-image pattern can sometimes only be identified at the subconscious level. In day-to-day conscious awareness, we might feel energetic, open, and ready to receive. Yet if the breath is shallow, part of us is resisting what we want, keeping it at bay.

Correcting this pattern requires a conscious effort to breathe more deeply and fully, remembering that the breath represents life and our "good" - what we really long for deep within ourselves. According to our capacity, the more oxygen we can bring into our bodies, the more good we can accept and experience in our lives. Once the old pattern releases and the new pattern takes over, the conscious effort is no longer required. Receiving becomes as natural a response as inhaling fully and freely has become.

Affirmations such as "I am worthy of prosperity and abundance," and "I accept my good fully and freely," are powerful agents of change in the subconscious mind, particularly when repeated silently while breathing deeply.

Now let's look at the exhalation. How we exhale represents how we handle negativity, in general, and our willingness to let go of what is no longer needed. For example, when breath analysis reveals vigorous blowing as we exhale, it is a sign of attempting to push negativity away, instead of simply letting it dissipate or leave our awareness.

This breathing pattern indicates a warrior personality, a fighter wanting to fight negativity. The problem with this pattern of living and breathing is that we actually draw into our lives whatever we focus our attention on. Trying to push something away tends to give it more power, making it come back even stronger. It's like a boomerang.

The biochemical correlation to this breathing pattern is a mild form of hyperventilation. When we blow the air out forcefully, we create an unnatural imbalance of oxygen and carbon dioxide in the body. Not surprisingly, warrior personalities tend to suffer regularly from anxiety and sometimes hyperventilate during the course of their often busy lives.

Another common pattern is controlling the exhalation by tightening muscles in the solar plexus and letting the breath out gradually. This represents the tendency to hold on to negativity. It could also translate into an overcontrolling personality, someone who tries to manipulate people and circumstances to avoid toppling the apple cart. The two problems correlate, certainly, since those holding on to unpleasant, negative thoughts and feelings frequently feel driven to control the external world in order to prevent more negative events from happening. The common denominator is a fixation on problems, or the negative, in life.

Learning just to let the breath go, in a relaxed, unvoiced flow establishes a relationship with life that enables us to deal with negativity in a healthier way. Letting it go quickly and gently, without trying to control or push it away, translates into peace of mind and surrender. The more we relax as we exhale and release toxins, the more we relax our hold on unhealthy behavior patterns. Relaxing as we exhale calms our physiology and tells the subconscious mind it is safe to let go of any worry, anger, or disappointment over unplanned circumstances. We are then free to take in the experience of the present moment and respond to it with full awareness.

One of the keys to gaining insight through breath analysis, then, is to observe the ratio of time spent inhaling to time spent exhaling. People who have a longer in-breath tend to focus on the positive things in life. Those with a longer out-breath typically dwell on the negative things in life. Therefore, if our intention is to receive more of what we consider good and positive, we focus on the inhalation. In a Transformational Breathing session we aim for an inhalation two to three times longer than the exhalation. Our intention is to breathe in as fully and openly as we can, naturally leading us to a freer, shorter, more relaxed exhale.

To the degree our breath is blocked and shut down, we block out the flow of life. But even if we have been limited by restricted breathing patterns our entire lives, these patterns can be overcome and changed in just a few sessions, and sometimes in just a few moments.

Aren't habits harder to change than that? With ordinary traditional methods, yes, they are. But Transformational Breathing works on levels beyond the conscious mind where time has little meaning. Beliefs can be reprogrammed in an instant—even the belief that says habits are hard to change!

Breathing Around the World

For many years, I assumed that the epidemic of dysfunctional breathing was a uniquely North American phenomenon, since my initial work was solely in the United States. It seemed to make sense that our cultural conditions and programming, which place such great emphasis on material wealth and technology over activities more closely aligned with nature, had perhaps squelched our capacity for natural, effective breathing.

In 1995, when I began sharing Transformational Breathing abroad, however, it became clear that restricted breathing is not unique to the US culture. And most interestingly, it also became apparent that the varying trends and conditions of different cultures can be readily identified in their breathing patterns.

I have since traveled to India, Germany, Russia, England, Italy, Taiwan, Mexico, Switzerland and Turkey, and plans are underway for journeys to Spain, Croatia, Holland, Belgium, South America, Canada and the Middle East. In each new country, common tendencies emerge among participants. My most in-depth experiences to date have taken place at conferences in Russia and professional training programs in England and Italy.

I was invited to present workshops at the International Free Breathers Conference in Moscow in 1997, and at the Spiritual Midwifery Conference in 1998. As a result of meeting and working with the Russian people, I noticed a unique synergistic balance between our cultures. I got the feeling that when Americans and Russians were together, we complemented each other in a number of ways. It seemed that we were like opposite sides of the same coin. The Russians were trained and conditioned towards unity or group consciousness. This teaches them to surrender their personal will for the good of the whole, yet often prevents the honoring of individual goals, rights, and higher purpose. In the United States, the focus has been more geared toward preserving individual freedom and expression. Our personal wills are much stronger. However, the majority of us seem to be almost unable to honor the good of the whole and unwilling to function with a sense of group consciousness. These attitudes are reflected in the way we breathe.

While in Russia, I worked with over four hundred individuals and found that about ninety percent of them were only breathing well in the upper chest. Throughout the training, we continually emphasized the importance of breathing into the belly, where personal will resides. Participants experienced real challenges trying to breathe into this area; slowly but surely, their natural breathing rhythms resurfaced. Eventually, as a result of the training, their personal wills grew stronger, and participants began expressing them more readily. They also reported much more awareness of who they were and what their lives were about.

I was amazed to find that these people, whom we Americans had been brought up to think of as the enemy, were so loving and expressive. Most were professionals—therapists, doctors, mid-wives, and breath-workers—eager to bring this knowledge and experience back to their clients and patients. We realized that we have much to offer each other, since our individual strengths and shortcomings are quite complementary. Together we seemed to balance the scales.

Freedoms and comforts many Americans take for granted are still only dreams for most Russians. Yet the freedom to breathe is something we can all share: when given the opportunity to open to the joy of their spirits with Transformational Breathing, the Russians responded with overwhelming appreciation and love.

After the workshops, participants lined up to share with me about how much the breathing had meant to them. They asked for pictures, autographs, and swore undying love and gratitude. Nowhere before had people expressed their appreciation for this work with such heartfelt emotion.

In the United States, I have not discovered any one predominant breathing pattern. We run pretty much across the board, reflecting the variety of our different heritages. However, there are some notable cultural differences between American men and women, which often show up in breath analysis.

Women, for example, are taught that we must have flat stomachs. Holding in the stomach and wearing certain items of clothing restricts breathing, particularly in the abdomen where the personal will is anchored in breath. Men are taught to hold their stomachs in, too, but more important is holding the chest out in order to look handsome and strong. This restricts the natural rise and fall of the chest area, where heartfelt feelings are stimulated by the flow of breath.

The English are quite conservative and guarded in expressing emotions. Breathing sessions gave them the opportunity to really become aware of their feelings, and usually revealed quite a buildup of repressed emotions in need of integration. Because the English are more reserved and emotionally inhibited, it was important to create a space where they felt safe to express themselves freely, both with me and with each other. This was also quite challenging!

Belly breathing is prevalent in England. This indicates a rather strong-willed and grounded approach to life. Most participants needed to open the upper respiratory system to more heart and love energy. This would liberate and rebalance their tendency to inhibit feelings.

For example, one day we went to a heated pool for an underwater breathing session with a mask and snorkel. The water experience seemed to stimulate the flow of emotions more dramatically than any other. In the United States, breathers typically move around a bit and make some muted sounds. The English group splashed and kicked around in the water like a pod of dolphins. The water environment often triggers early memories of being in the womb, which can be very intense emotionally. However, the degree of expressive activity from this delightful group was more pronounced than in any other I have seen, which indicated to me how much emotional repression they had built up.

Italy presented another unique set of patterns and characteristics. Many Italian breathers had little or no breath going to the lower respiratory system. This indicated a lack of physical grounding and less development of the personal will. Considering the political and religious environments in Italy, my guess is that a good deal of personal will and expression has been abdicated to the church and state.

Normally, one out of every hundred clients may gag or vomit a little bit during a breathing session. This is often experienced as stuffed or gagged emotions or a reenactment of the necessary purging of fluid from the lungs just after birth. In Italy, the incidence of this was far greater. Sometimes as many as ten or more in each group session would be going through not only emotional upheavals but physical ones as well.

In Taiwan, I noticed that women had extremely restricted breath capacity in the upper chest and throat. This only makes sense when you realize how the culture has historically repressed the self-expression of women. Lots of choking and coughing ensued during the breathing sessions in Asia, typically followed by reports of openings to greater expression of self and feelings.

As Transformational Breathing continues to spread across the planet, I find it fascinating to witness the symbolic meanings of cultural breathing patterns. It is even more inspiring to see how easily those restricted patterns can change.

Ironically, the cultural differences that so often seem to divide us actually do create balance and wholeness in the world. With Transformational Breathing, more and more people are finding that a similar balance exists within themselves.

Perhaps Norman Lear said it best: "If we could pull all the

peoples of the world into one room and put them through the experience I had with Transformational Breathing, the world would be a much better place."

Once we release the perceived need to walk our own tightropes, there is nothing to defend. Perceived cultural differences are no longer threatening, and there can be no enemy. Breath by breath, we bring wholeness, and the awareness of our deep interconnection, not only to each individual breather, but also to the entire planet.

*"The breath is
the movement
of Spirit
in the body."*

Andrew Weil, MD

6

Breathing into
Body, Mind, and Spirit

We've all heard a great deal about the body/mind/spirit connection over the past decade. What are these three aspects of humanity, and how do they affect each other? While it is probably impossible to answer that question to everyone's satisfaction, we can discuss some basics as they apply to breathing.

Have you ever stopped to notice what you are saying when you refer to your body? If *it* is your body, then *what* are *you*? I hurt my ankle. Is my ankle me? No. Who am I? I am the observer. As my friend and colleague Dr. Deepak Chopra likes to say, "I am not a physical being having an occasional spiritual experience. I am a spiritual being having an occasional physical experience."

The physical body might be considered a very high-tech vehicle that we earth-dwelling spirits get to drive around in order to experience life in a way that is very different from simply being our energetic-intelligent selves. Yet every single cell of our bodies shares in and expresses our innate intelligence. The problem is that once we are associated with a body, by being born with one, we tend to get so enthralled with learning to drive this magnificent vehicle that we forget we are the *driver*, not the vehicle.

This forgetting is valuable and necessary as we learn to drive and maintain our vehicle. But once we've mastered the basics, we're ready for our great journey: remembering who the driver is and recreating ourselves, in each moment, to be truly magnificent. Reevaluating and relearning basic bodily functions are major stepping-stones along the way.

What is Mind? In keeping with our vehicular metaphor, mind is the steering wheel. It's the tool we use to steer and operate the body. Mind is also like the software, which controls various functions of the vehicle, and the programmer, who creates new ways to communicate through it. The mind interprets input and decides whether and how to express output. The mind gathers up information, stores it for later use and retrieves it when the need arises. The mind is the great copilot or indispensable executive secretary organizing the driving experience and coordinating the linkage between driver and vehicle (you and your body).

Two primary aspects of mind are the conscious and subconscious. The conscious mind is the part that is aware of yourself thinking, and the subconscious mind is the hidden storage unit, of which the conscious mind is not usually aware. The conscious mind might be compared to the user of a computer who has specific goals for its use and navigates through the software programs to get the job done. The subconscious mind is better compared to the basic operating system of a computer, of which the user rarely is aware, but without which the software could not function. It keeps all the background functions and files working and records everything that occurs from the moment it was created. If files are not deleted from time to time and system maintenance is not performed regularly, bits of information get fragmented and a crash is inevitable.

A third aspect of mind is our superconscious or transcendent mind. This is the part of the mind that communicates directly with Divine Mind or Spirit.

What is Spirit? Perhaps the simplest way to define spirit is to say that it is the core essence of who we are. It is the intelligent energy that animates our minds and bodies.

When any one of the members of this grand triad—body, mind and spirit—insists that something external is more important than the balance of the triad itself, trouble ensues. Imbalance and disharmony gradually disintegrate into conflict and illness, both within ourselves and with others. Transformational Breathing can serve to scan and reintegrate the operating system, restoring balance within the triad.

As discussed earlier, breathing is the one subconscious metabolic function that we can claim as the conscious mind's domain whenever we so choose. Our breathing gives us an important passkey to the control room of the subconscious mind, which can get too big for its britches! It can start to act like Hal, the computer control system that went haywire and started making executive decisions for the entire spaceship in Stanley Kubrick's 1960s science-fiction movie, *2001: A Space Odyssey.* If you don't remember the movie, just imagine a computer in an office that suddenly decides it knows best, and is going to run the business!

If left to its own devices, the subconscious mind can become the driving force in your life. You end up feeling like a back seat driver, wondering how you ended up in this mess—and the next one. Since we know our conscious choices didn't get us there, we frequently start looking outside ourselves for someone or something else to blame. At this point, the hopeless-victim mentality often kicks into overdrive. An endless race to an imaginary finish line ensues, with all the stress and frustration of a bad dream.

Conscious breathing is a surefire way to take the reins back and start creating what you want in your life, instead of letting the subconscious mind continue to recreate, over and over again, what it has experienced in the past. There is a simple yet profound axiom found in popular Twelve-Step recovery programs: "If you always do what you've always done, you'll always get what you've always gotten." Taking conscious control of our breath mechanism is the most powerful—and easiest—place to start doing things differently.

Since Transformational Breathing works on all three levels—body, mind, and spirit—one passes through all of these levels, or stages, in any given breathing session. Each level corresponds to different kinds of processes and benefits. While it can be helpful to address each level separately, the three are not truly separate, but comprise the interdependent whole that is you. With every conscious and unconscious breath we take, all three levels of our being are affected, and choosing to breathe consciously supports complete healing and integration.

Integration is the blending together, or reunion, of our physical, mental, and spiritual aspects, to create wholeness, balance, and harmony. Until these elements of ourselves act, speak, and think in unison with full acceptance of each other, we are fragmented, unbalanced, and off kilter. As we merge these aspects of self, full integrity is easy to uphold, since we are better equipped to express our whole truth without fear. Our own innate joy, and the love we long to share, can then be free to permeate and transform our lives.

When the breath becomes a conscious tool, we can liberate ourselves from past experiences and all associated emotions. We can use it to master our everyday mental and emotional states. We gain the power to choose our thoughts, and therefore our feelings, instead of being held hostage to outdated subconscious archives.

Conscious breathing gives us the instant ability to bridge the gap between the conscious and unconscious worlds, providing a most profound way to realize the truth about our higher purpose on Earth. Bringing such truth to light gives birth to thoughts and feelings that naturally guide us to fulfill our purpose.

Level 1: Opening the Breath

Let's pretend for a moment that we're suddenly plopped into the vehicle of our dreams. We'll use all our senses to describe it in the finest detail. What does it look like? Feel like? Smell like? I'm getting a yellow Rolls Royce convertible with green leather interior. How about it? What's yours?

This dream car is brand-spanking new and all yours; you just brought it home today. How will you take care of it? Will you polish it up an hour after getting it home? Take it for a ride in the country? Lend anyone else the keys? Or will you put sugar in the tank? Water in the engine? Oil in the radiator? Of course not. It's premium gasoline and kid gloves for this beauty all the way.

Now take a look at your lifelong vehicle—your body. This is the vehicle of your soul's dreams, and it's permanent—no trade-ins this century. No lemon laws. Isn't it just as important as your dream car? Just as valuable? Wasn't your spirit just thrilled to slide into such an ingenious and sensitively prepared physical body so you could touch, taste, love, and create?

Like our cars, our bodies need proper care and maintenance, and to help our bodies serve us well, we must first open up our restricted, closed-down breathing patterns.

Most people think that as long as they breathe in and out once in a while, they are doing fine. The truth is, however, that unless we frequently breathe deeply and fully every day, our bodies are not getting the oxygen needed for good health. In fact, some of us do not take in enough air even for minimal health. There's an epidemic of sub-ventilators in our culture, which explains many of society's ills.

The need for oxygen is so basic and pervasive that I cannot write enough about it. Every physical and chemical process of the body requires oxygen; every cell in the body needs a continuous supply to function with maximal benefit. If our breathing is shallow and ineffective, our oxygen intake will be insufficient, and changes, diseases, and malfunctions can occur on a cellular level. Obviously, using our full respiratory system allows us to give our bodies the oxygen they need to stay healthy and strong.

Many major diseases are the direct or indirect result of insufficient oxygen supplied to the body. In Nathaniel Altman's book, *Oxygen Healing Therapies for Optimum Health and Vitality,* he cites more than fifty diseases, maladies and immune disorders successfully treated in Russia, Cuba, Mexico, and Germany with various oxygen therapies.

As Altman explains, "The primary effect that breathing has on the body is oxidation, a natural process that involves oxygen combining with another substance. As a result, the chemical composition of both substances changes. Oxidation occurs as combustion within the body when oxygen turns sugar into energy. Our body also uses oxidation as its first line of defense against harmful bacteria, viruses, yeasts, and parasites. Oxidizing molecules attack the pathogenic cells and they are removed from the body through its normal processes of elimination.

"After oxidation, the most important function of breathing is oxygenation—saturation with oxygen—as in the aeration of blood in the lungs. When poor oxygenation is chronic, our overall immune response to germs and viruses is weakened, making us vulnerable to a wide range of diseases."

With every organ and cell dependent upon oxygen-rich blood for nourishment, the blood's quality depends largely upon proper oxygenation of the lungs. If under-oxygenated, the blood becomes laden with impurities, including carbon monoxide, which poisons cells and weakens the immune system. When it remains as an uneliminated waste product in the blood, disease develops.

Our bodies need between six and eight pounds of oxygen each day. Ideally, the air should contain at least twenty percent oxygen. However, due to air pollution, mostly from factory and automobile exhausts and burning garbage, combined with the

severe reduction of the earth's oxygen-producing trees and rain
forests, oxygen levels can be as low as ten percent in some cities.
The depletion of oxygen in the atmosphere was verified by archae-
ologists when air bubbles trapped in ancient amber, as well as in
core samples of ice from Polar Regions, were found to contain
twice the oxygen levels found in present-day air.

Could oxygen be the most important anti-carcinogen known
to modern man? Two-time Nobel Laureate Dr. Otto Warburg
proved that cancer cells live by fermentation. They are anaerobic
and, therefore, can only proliferate where cells are getting little or
no oxygen. Their degenerative nature influences the cells around
them as well. Dr. Warburg discovered that if you deprive a cell of
sixty percent of its oxygen, it will turn cancerous. This has been
instrumental in recent treatments for cancer and other incurable
diseases.

Co-enzyme Q-10, germanium, lipoic acid, aloe vera, ozone
therapies, and hyperbaric oxygen chambers, just to name a few, all
ultimately increase levels of usable oxygen to the cells. In a variety
of roundabout ways, these and other amazingly curative substances affect the body's supply and/or demand for oxygen.

A far more cost-effective approach is establishing a habit of
full, open breathing. In addition to the benefits of increased oxygen
levels in the blood, more endorphins, adrenaline, neuropeptides,
insulin, and other beneficial chemicals are released into our system
as well, resulting in elevated emotional states and mental clarity.
Full, conscious breathing is the most natural, safe, effective and
affordable oxygen therapy available today.

Symptoms of disease are messages from the body/mind to
alert us to imbalances or, literally, lack of ease (dis-ease). When
the conscious mind receives and understands the message,
symptoms sometimes disappear spontaneously. More often, such
understanding leads to behavior changes and therapeutic measures to resolve the problem. If we ignore these messages, more
serious disease takes hold of our lives.

When we breathe consciously, we enlarge our perspective
and can better understand and resolve the conditions of discomfort
and disease. Meanwhile, the increased oxygen supply is doing its
part to rebalance our physical biochemistry. It's quite a powerful

combination.

One of the most obvious benefits of opening up breathing patterns and establishing new ones is the improvement of respiratory and bronchial conditions. Good healthy lung tissue resists disease, and the only way to have healthy tissue is to use the lungs properly.

In addition to the obvious benefits of strengthening the respiratory muscles and bringing in more oxygen to heal the lung tissue, full diaphragmatic breathing also activates the area of the lungs where the highest concentration of alveoli wait for oxygen. Alveoli are the tiny microscopic sacs that absorb and distribute oxygen to red blood cells as they pass through with each pulse of the heart. If we are not breathing with the help of our most important respiratory muscle, the diaphragm, we are not pulling the oxygen deeply enough into the lungs to take advantage of our most abundant exchange program. Yawning can help with this problem to some degree, but why not learn to use these eager little sacs more readily?

Studies have shown that heart patients who learn diaphragmatic breathing significantly improve the health of their hearts. The fact that hypertension and anxiety can be relieved with conscious breathing has also been proven through research.

Alan Hymes, M.D., co-author of *Science of Breath: A Practical Guide,* writes, "Essential hypertension (high blood pressure of unknown cause) has been shown to respond favorably to a daily regimen of diaphragmatic breathing. This is especially encouraging when one considers the number of deaths per year in the U.S. from heart disease alone that are associated with hypertension. Diaphragmatic breathing, in conjunction with relaxation exercises, has resulted in impressive improvements in treating anxiety states in at least one study, and this represents a mode of treatment free from the potential side effects of medications." In a number of private sessions with clients who had high blood pressure, I measured blood pressure before and after the session. In each case there was at least a ten-point decrease after the breathing.

A diaphragm is a horizontal sheet of muscle or fascia that moves during breathing. Based on this definition, there is more than one diaphragm in the body. In fact, there are eight of them. These horizontal sheets of muscle are connected together continuously by vertical sheets of fascia. This interconnected system enables our diaphragms to move in synchrony during breathing.

Since nearly all of the organs in the body are hanging from or resting on a diaphragm, they are all moved and pumped with each breath, aiding the flow of fluids throughout the organs. This means that all types of fluid transport are improved: arterial, venous, lymphatic, nerve, and extracellular. As fluid transport is improved, the amount of nutrients delivered and the quantity of wastes removed is increased.

Detoxification is another important benefit of proper breathing. As much as seventy percent of the toxins we take in each day, as well as those already stored in the body, can be eliminated through the breath. Any knowledgeable doctor will confirm that bad breath is often a result of toxins being carried out through exhalation. Does this mean you should keep your mouth shut so as not to drive away neighbors, friends, and lovers? Quite the contrary. Therapeutic breath sessions will detoxify your system *and* motivate you toward more nontoxic *and* detoxifying habits. Many conscious breathers find it easy to quit smoking, drinking, and taking drugs, and tend to become attracted to healthier foods as well.

Considering all these benefits of conscious breathing, it is easy to see how improving our breathing efficiency can increase health and vitality. Natural healing often occurs during the breath session as tensions from the mind/body are resolved and released. In addition to being a powerful healing tool, Transformational Breathing complements and strengthens all other forms of healing and therapy.

Let's summarize the overall biological benefits of optimal respiration. By increasing vital oxygen levels in the body, effective breathing helps balance the blood pH, reduce hypertension, clear toxins out of the system, strengthen the immune system, and vastly increase energy levels. It also improves memory function, metabolic activity, and muscle and vascular tone (particularly of the diaphragms), and assists lymphatic drainage, arterial blood flow, and psychological functioning via brain chemistry. How's that for starters?

"When you breathe
you ignite the subtle
vibration of Joy.
Let the joy build
in your bodies
as you breathe."

Vywamus

The Electromagnetic Body

The nervous system is adversely affected by inadequate breathing. The brain, spinal cord, nerve centers, and nerves themselves all become poor and inefficient instruments for generating, storing, and transmitting nerve currents (electrical impulses) if the blood is oxygen-poor. Oxygen is an essential ingredient in the production of cellular chemical energy. It is through the oxygenation and charging of these nerve currents that we receive our vital Life Force energy.

As mentioned earlier, up to seventy-five percent of the effective energy we need in order to function comes from breathing. In the course of twenty-four hours, the average adult male consumes about seven or eight pounds of oxygen, four pounds of food and two pounds of water. Although the quality and quantity of Life Force in the food and water we consume is significant, together it is less than half of that received through oxygen intake. The red blood cells are responsible for delivering the oxygen throughout the body, and certain other nutrients, derived from food, are essential in this process.

Perhaps the flow of oxygen in our bodies is identical to the flow of Life Force or *prana*. Prana is the ancient Sanskrit term used in Eastern philosophical texts, which are the original written sources for our earliest collective knowledge about breathing.

Yogis speak of prana in the air. They say it is everywhere, with some places having more than others. In the words of Swami Rama, the renowned yogi who offered his amazing mastery of his own body and the physical world to be studied extensively by

Western scientists, "Prana is the vital link between mind and body, and breath is the vehicle for prana. Prana enlivens matter... It is primal energy; "pra" meaning *first* and "na" meaning *unit* or *energy*." The closest English translation for prana is Life Force.

The Life Force energy enters our bodies via the breath, sunlight exposure, and the ingestion of water and raw foods. It is then converted to cellular fuel for biological processes. The energy received through our oxygen intake is not only biochemical but also electromagnetic.

Studies conducted by West German physicist Johanna Budwig, Ph.D., demonstrate the interplay between biochemical and electromagnetic forces in the body, while presenting some interesting facts about the role of related nutrients. "The red blood cells in the lungs drop off carbon dioxide and take on oxygen. The oxygen-laden cells are then transported to the cell site where they release their oxygen into the plasma. This newly released oxygen is attracted to the cells by the resonance of the "pi-electron" of oxidation-enhancing fatty acids. Without the electrical charge of these fatty acids, oxygen cannot work its way into the cell."

Her technical papers, dating as far back as 1951, proved that electron-rich fatty acids play a defining role in "respiratory enzymes, which are the basis of cell oxidation." She further states that these electron-rich fats "resonate with the wavelength of the sun's light and control the entire scope of our bodies' vital life functions."

For some, it is uncomfortable to think about that ineffable borderland between the material or physical world and the invisible energetic realm. Yet who knows how real that border is? It may simply come down to different ways of talking about the same processes or different levels of perception.

According to the brilliant Albert Einstein, perhaps the best-known scientist of Western civilization, nothing is "unquestionably physical." This is because all matter—solid, liquid, and gas—is made up of tiny atomic and subatomic particles separated by relatively huge amounts of space compared to their size. Gases have more space between particles than do solids, because gas particles vibrate at a higher frequency. The largest of these particles are protons, neutrons, and electrons. These are composed of even smaller particles, also held together by energy, with relatively large distances between them.

Thus, we are composed mostly of space with particles vibrating in it. This vibration is caused by the push and pull of magnetic energy, invisible, yet powerful. Consider the pull of a magnet. Can you see or feel what pulls it toward metal?

Every cell in our body is electrically charged, like a tiny magnet. Even the tiniest atoms of a cell are charged. The proton carries a positive charge and the electron a negative charge. Neutrons are neutral. Furthermore, we all have our own electromagnetic field—a variety of energy patterns fluctuating at various wavelengths.

Physicists have determined that the denser an object appears and feels, the more slowly are its atoms vibrating (or spinning, as some prefer to describe it). This rate of vibration is called frequency. Sounds, colors, thoughts, actions, plastic, bricks, balloons, baseballs, humans, dolphins, snakes, and swing sets— all these function exactly the same at the most elemental level. All are made up of the same stuff: energy—electrons, protons and neutrons—yet all are vibrating at different frequencies. These unique energy frequencies cause each item to display a separate set of perceptible characteristics and qualities with which our senses can play.

The most modern theories on how matter/energy behaves have grand metaphysical implications with respect to energy and physical reality. This is especially true of Einstein's theory of relativity and the interplay of the observer and the observed. Simply stated, whenever an object is observed, it is affected by the observer, presumably due to the interplay of their energy fields.

The scientific principle of entrainment states that when a high-frequency energy field is introduced to a low-frequency energy pattern for a period of time, the latter is compelled to match, or more closely resemble, the higher frequency.

Have you ever noticed the heavy, dense sensation that usually accompanies unpleasant feelings such as grief, depression, or resentment? It's as if you desperately want to shake a weight off your shoulders. Feelings are forms of energy too. Those heavy feelings and emotions are made up of energy patterns, which are vibrating at a lower frequency than pleasant feelings such as love, humor, and joy. Think back to a time when you had a good belly laugh with a close friend. Do you remember the feeling of lightness and levity, or even a high sensation? Remember the floating feeling of witnessing a child being born, or melting into a first kiss. Notice how just thinking about various feelings causes us to feel heavier or lighter. This is due to the fact that unpleasant feelings exist in our body-mind as lower-frequency energy patterns and pleasant feelings exist as higher-frequency patterns. Therefore, if we raise our frequencies, we automatically increase the awareness of joy in our lives.

If you are having a hard time believing that feelings exist as energy in your body, consider the medical practice of measuring the electrical energy frequencies called brain waves. Or think about how a lie detector test clearly demonstrates measurable physiological responses to our thoughts and feelings. While the subject is answering specific questions, electrodes hooked up to the body are busy reading its electrical impulses. The energy frequency of a truthful response is dramatically different from that of a lie.

Entrainment is a scientifically documented principle of the energetic relationships between things, and their influences upon one another. Again, when a high-frequency energy pattern maintains close contact with a low-frequency energy pattern for a period of time, the lower frequency will be caused to permanently increase its rate of vibration to match or more closely resemble the higher frequency.

As stated, breathing brings in prana, which has a very high vibrational frequency. An open, full, and connected breath, which does not pause after inhalation or exhalation, establishes a "luminous sphere," or closed circuit, of continuing high-frequency energy in our own electromagnetic field. This energy pattern stimulates feelings of joy, gratitude, and love, which can make a breathing session quite pleasant. However, just as opposite magnetic poles attract, these higher, lighter energies cause that which is *not* joy, gratitude, or love to come into our awareness as well. As lower-frequency energies such as anger, grief, hatred, or guilt come into full contact with the higher-frequency energies, they entrain to the higher frequency. The energies do not leave. We are not actually getting rid of anything. They simply transform into the higher frequency of energy, which we experience as lighter feelings. This state of lightness ultimately gives us higher levels of energy to use in creating what we *will*.

Entrainment can be witnessed in many everyday relationships. Imagine a room full of pendulum clocks all moving in different rhythmic patterns. Within a short period of time, they begin to swing in unison. A mother and nursing infant provide another example of entrainment, as their heartbeats synchronize. Groups of women, living or working together, often find their menstrual cycles coincide over time. Sound waves and various pitches entrain other energy fields so effectively that an entire healing science has developed based on using sound to entrain disruptive energy patterns.

Naturally, better breathing translates into increased energy, since increased energy comes from the high vibration of prana, or Life Force, and from the physical oxygenation of our cells and tissues (assuming these are different processes). Even one adjustment in someone's breathing pattern can double or triple their energy level and vitality. The solution to feeling tired all the time can be as simple as consciously redirecting the breathing pattern and retraining respiratory muscles. In addition, when old repressed emotions, negative thought forms, and energy blockages—all lower vibrational energy patterns that can result in physical disease—are entrained and integrated into higher, healthier frequencies, overall health is enhanced.

There is one way of breathing that is
shameful and constricted.
Then there is another way;
A breath of love that takes you
all the way to infinity.

Rumi

9

Level 2: Freeing the Mind

One of the primary keys to happiness is managing our own thoughts. Thoughts are a very fertile form of energy, the seeds from which everything in life grows. Our life is like a garden, and it needs tending. If we don't step up and plant our chosen seeds, pull the weeds, and nurture the plants we want around, somebody else will. Who will it be?

If you are now experiencing difficulty in your life, chances are you have not been tending your own garden of thoughts. Who has been? Parents, TV characters, friends, newscasters, neighbors, teachers, religious leaders? If we allow others to plant and fertilize the seeds of their choosing in our garden, is it any wonder that poison ivy pops up instead of roses? We have given someone else the power to germinate their thoughts in our lives.

In order to get the garden we want, we have to tend it ourselves. We must take responsibility for choosing which seeds to plant. Our thoughts are those seeds. Positive, loving intent and words provide the sunshine, and acting with integrity provides the water. We must plant these seeds, give them sunlight, water them, and pull out any weeds that might otherwise overrun our lives.

The subconscious mind might be compared to a garden of perennials planted years ago by parents and other authority figures as we were growing up. Many subconscious thoughts come up over and over again, without any effort. Even if we try to plant new seedlings in their place, the roots of the perennial thoughts are going to come up. What we need is a good rototilling to grind those roots into mulch, which can then be used to fertilize and energize the new growth. Transformational Breathing is just such a rototiller, drilling to the very depths of our subconscious mind to root out and transform negativity into fertile soil for healthy thoughts.

Wilhelm Reich, M.D., founder of the Reichian approach to psychotherapy, was one of the first in his field to clearly stress that "emotional and physical states can be altered by changing the breathing patterns."

This may have a great deal to do with the activity of the eight diaphragms mentioned earlier. According to Scott Kwiatkowski, D.O., "Emotional tension is most often stored on or next to a diaphragm, thereby restricting breathing patterns. Therefore it is important for emotional and physical health that all the diaphragms are moving freely and in sync with the breath."

The breath holds the key to healing our mental health because we can consciously change our chemistry as well as attitude by changing the depth, rhythm, and rate of our breathing. As we make these changes, our perspectives and attitudes are altered to engage a more positive mind-body state, thereby dramatically improving our sense of well-being. Not only does increased oxygen improve alertness and mental clarity of the physical brain and conscious mind, it also accesses the subconscious mind, efficiently healing and permanently resolving the roots of stored negativity and suppressed emotions. On these deeper emotional levels, Transformational Breathing results in the integration of suppressions and the permanent clearing of negativity from the subconscious mind.

First, it is important to understand the significant role that physical birth plays in shaping our core belief patterns and therefore our entire approach to life. Because birth is our first experience on the physical plane, we tend to formulate many ideas at that time of the nature of life in this world. What we experience at birth, and how we respond to it, sets up and influences many of our lifelong emotions, attitudes, and behaviors. These continue to multiply in layers upon one another, throughout our lives, unless the original imprints are reframed and transformed.

Fortunately, the traumatic experience of birth, and its reverberations throughout life, are some of the first issues to surface during conscious breathing sessions. Like Rebirthing, Transformational Breathing helps us to access our own birth memories and clear away the false impressions about life that we assumed from that initial experience of breathing.

For example, we may have been treated roughly by the physician attending our birth—perhaps even turned upside down and spanked on the bottom, which was the usual hospital practice for many years. Considering the power of first impressions, this could easily lead to the assumption that men—or authority figures—are rough and abusive. Based on that belief, we manifest cycle after cycle of similar experiences that confirm the original belief.

The human mind has a strong drive to prove itself right. Our beliefs create feelings and experiences that support and strengthen the original beliefs. These feelings and experiences in turn create another layer of life experience and so on in a spiraling cycle. Transformational Breathing can access our core beliefs, truly transform them, and break the cycle of negative behavior and experience.

Core beliefs are stored in the subconscious mind, which can be divided into two levels. The lower subconscious consists of the emotional body and the subliminal mind, the part of which we're not aware. Everything we have ever experienced is stored here like a computer file. There is no discernment between types of information; the lower subconscious simply accepts and records everything, whether we are awake and aware or not. No wonder there are layers upon layers of suppressed false negativity to clear at this level!

The higher subconscious mind (sometimes called the superconscious or non-local mind) is not fully understood and still considered by many to be a great mystery. Some feel that all the knowledge of the universe is accessible at this level.

These two parts of the subconscious together account for much of our mental activity, from dreams to intuition to autonomic function. Although many people ignore the subconscious mind and remain oblivious to its not-so-subtle effects on the body and mental state, this form of ignorance does not lead to bliss. Clearing it does.

Let's take a moment to define the distinction between suppressions and repressions, both of which reside in the lower subconscious mind. Suppressions are emotions that have been "sent to the dungeon" after a conscious decision to do so. For example, you hold your tongue and keep your mouth shut when being chewed out by your boss, even though you might really like to jump in his face and tell him what a control freak he is. You consciously choose to suppress your feelings in that moment.

Repressions, on the other hand, are emotions that never see the light of day—they are automatically sent to the dungeon without a hearing. They are used sometimes as an unconscious defense mechanism to help us survive. Repressions are usually the result of unpleasant experiences in early infancy and childhood, for example, a traumatic first day in kindergarten. Even at that age, we had already learned that certain kinds of feelings were just not safe to have and had become unconsciously competent at denying their existence and expression.

(*Note:* For simplicity's sake, throughout this book, I'll use the word *repression* to represent both forms of stuffed emotions or feelings.)

Repressed emotions have a strong impact upon our breathing, our bodies, and our lives. In order to keep the imprisoned feelings from escaping, we must habitually arrest and confine our respiratory system. Cut off from our primary source of energy, we do not receive enough oxygen for even the basic physical demands of life. We become disconnected from our bodies, sometimes unaware of even the *possibility* of pleasant feelings. Keeping these doors of expression closed requires a tremendous amount of energy and creates chronic tension, particularly in the respiratory muscles. This all translates into chronic stress, or worse. This is where disease is manufactured: in the dark dungeon of denial.

The lower subconscious exerts a powerful influence on our beliefs, attitudes, and emotions because of the negative repressed experiences and thoughts stored there. Yet we are often oblivious to their detrimental influence on our lives. The nature and function of the lower subconscious is to help us survive by denying or separating ourselves from unacceptable or overwhelming feelings and thoughts. When these painful or unpleasant events occur, we withdraw our awareness from them and pay attention to other things. While initially this denial can help us survive and grow, eventually it can become a huge barrier to our experiencing life directly and fully.

Although holding the breath effectively seems to deactivate unacceptable feelings, these feelings don't disappear because we consciously deny them. They merely take up space in a deeper level of our consciousness and become part of our "emotional energy body." By repressing memories and emotions in an attempt to avoid dealing with them, we end up paying very high rental fees for storage in the subconscious mind. The currency with which we pay that debt is called joy. If you can't remember what unconditional joy feels like, you may have gone emotionally bankrupt from paying this price. Some refer to this as spiritual bankruptcy.

There are physical as well as mental aspects to this stored energy. Every cell in our body has a memory, and trauma and negativity also get stored at this cellular, physical level. Unless we are able to access and shift the energy of the subconscious, it all remains there as a perceptual filter through which we continue to experience our life, affecting our ability to perceive it in a clear, present manner.

Think how often people stuff their feelings and flee from painful experiences and emotions based on fearful, judgmental thoughts. Remember when you were growing up how rarely you were encouraged to express your feelings? All the times you were told to be quiet? Not to be afraid? Not to see it your way? Add in all the limiting cultural conditioning and media programming, such as "women can't do that," "big boys don't cry," "sunlight causes cancer," and "ninety percent of us will get the flu this year." It is easy to see how layers and layers of self-limiting beliefs are reinforced. And it is no wonder we've created deep pockets of unconsciousness to contain it all.

Whether we are aware of it or not, this unresolved negativity weighs us down, leading to ever-increasing heaviness in mind and body, more undesirable experiences, and self-limiting, self-sabotaging behaviors. In order to keep our locked-up feelings from escaping, we habitually clamp down on our respiratory system throughout the day.

The good news is that we can use this same breath to access the subconscious and clear repressed feelings and memories, without having to consciously analyze (or in many cases even be aware of) each and every one of them. We can assist cellular restoration by clearing past memories at the cellular level through vibrational entrainment. In further assisting the process of entrainment, the breath works to liberate old energies and stored emotions by physically re-awakening key areas of the respiratory system that are being poorly utilized.

Every part of the respiratory system harbors specific kinds of emotions. When we repeatedly withdraw our awareness from a feeling or perhaps substitute another, we also stop breathing into the part of the respiratory system where that particular emotion tends to reside. We can tap into these areas again by deliberately allowing our breath to enter them, thereby accessing the emotions stored there.

As we continue to breathe into these closed places, we must also give ourselves permission to feel whatever is evoked. Crying is our natural and primary vehicle for the release of intense unpleasant feelings (or pain). It works based on the same basic principles of breathing: the exhaling of toxins, and the inhaling of cleansing oxygen. Unexpressed physical pain, emotional anguish, grief, and trauma all create toxic stress, which can be measured as both chemical excretions and energetic changes. Crying aloud releases and expresses toxic feelings. This occurs energetically through verbal sound frequencies and chemically through exhalation.

Tears also carry toxins out of the system and cleanse the retina, leading to better, clearer vision afterward. Have you ever noticed how babies, who are usually allowed to cry without being shamed, seem so completely at peace once the crying subsides? Perhaps you remember a time when you allowed yourself to cry fully, without holding back. Remember the feelings of lightness and clarity that emerged after the tears were dried and breathing returned to normal?

The natural expulsion of sound and breath helps to move out that intense pain energy. It eliminates the excess adrenaline and other secretions dumped into the system as "fight or flight" bio-chemical reactions. The inhaling phase of a good, wracking sob refills the resulting void with more of the good stuff: vital, cleansing oxygen—pure Life Force. Unfortunately, it is common in our modern culture to forbid, or at least discourage, this natural cleansing process. Most of us at one time or another have tried to comfort a child, friend or loved one by saying, "Don't cry."

Men are doubly burdened with the stigma of crying. After all, "It's not manly to cry." And don't forget, "Boys who cry are sissies." This could be one reason why many men feel more out of touch with their feelings than do women. Women are less forbidden to cry, although still sometimes shamed, particularly by men. When faced with a woman or a child who is crying, a man may get inklings of his own buried feelings attempting to find their own route of expression in the throat. But he has been firmly trained to keep those expressions from occurring. Instead of allowing himself to cry, a man often switches to anger, the more acceptable male emotion, and demands that the crying stop.

Because we are so fervently taught that crying is not an acceptable behavior, we begin to hold our breath when stressful situations arise. Allowing the breath to go unchecked would naturally lead to crying or screaming. We learn that holding our breath helps us to avoid feeling anything that is potentially painful or uncomfortable, either to ourselves or to those around us.

Consider what would happen to your health if you refused to relieve your bladder or bowels when the need arose. Crying is simply another natural bodily function ingeniously designed for eliminating toxins. Yet, as a society, we have assigned it to the realm of shameful taboo.

Is it absolutely necessary to cry? Is crying the only way to release these trapped emotional energy patterns? No. It is a gift when we allow ourselves to cry. Transformational Breathing is also a gift. It is a highly effective method for integrating emotions as they arise, with or without tears.

In the same way that we repress painful emotions, we also

learn to repress our joy. Children are often told to be quiet when laughing. Although laughter is more acceptable than crying, it's not always okay to laugh loudly. We learn that laughing is only permitted at certain times, in certain places, and at certain volumes.

There are many seemingly good reasons, at the time, for parents to demand silence instead of laughter. I remember when the minister at church had toilet paper stuck on his shoe. Mom spent most of the mass angrily stifling my giggles. It was not nice, I was told. And then there was the time when the boy I had a crush on in school broke wind in class. I thought it was hilarious. The principal did not.

Laughing heartily is another wonderful way to move the energy of breath through us vigorously, and it's so much fun!

A full belly laugh works in much the same way crying does: a deep breath in, followed by a relaxed breath out releases tension and toxins and exercises our favorite abdominal muscle, the diaphragm. The physiology is similar, but the conscious experience is quite different. The end result of both is the experience of more joy.

Not surprisingly, studies have shown that laughter is very healing. The story of the amazing recovery of Norman Cousins from a crippling illness instigated some of those studies. In his book, *Anatomy of an Illness,* he describes how he watched comedy movies literally for days, laughed himself silly, and got well.

Transformational Breathing allows most people once again to experience the free flow of emotions as they did in early childhood. They stop judging their experience and more readily accept all feelings and forms of emotional expression in the safe setting of a breath session. Those who suffer from boiling anger and rage finally find welcome relief. Parents tend to become more tolerant and open to their children's need to laugh and to cry. Laughing freely, expressing feelings becomes acceptable and a welcome joy.

This shift alone leads to more fun and better health. It is far healthier to feel the feeling, welcoming it into our experience, than to stuff it down indefinitely. With full and open breathing, we release the hauntingly pervasive influences of the past and reclaim our inherent right to a full range of emotions We gain the freedom to live fully in the present moment without our emotional history dictating our reaction to each new experience. This is one of the ultimate rewards of Transformational Breathing.

"Fear is excitement without the breath."

Fritz Perls, M.D.

10

Level 3: Reclaiming Our True Nature

What is our true nature? Are we more than a body, mind, and feelings? Is there a deeper part of our being we have yet to explore? Many of us encounter a good deal of fear when we think about exploring the deeper, less dimensions of reality. Perhaps this fear of the unknown was programmed into our minds at a very young age, often for seemingly valid reasons.

To transform means, "to go beyond form." In Transformational Breathing, we are not going into worlds beyond. We are going into worlds within, where we find our true nature and discover the spiritual side of life.

Once false, self-limiting judgments and their resulting emotions are cleared, we can better access the lighter states of love, peace, and joy, which reflect our true nature. These states are always within us, but are often overridden by the influence of repressed energies and outmoded beliefs. As those old feelings are light-washed by the high-frequency energy of the Transformational Breathing, we begin to experience our limitless spiritual nature more vividly.

Now the door is open to connect with the Soul, resulting in an increased capacity to experience more fully the superconscious self and the higher-dimensional aspects of existence. This can lead to mystical experiences, great insight, and enhanced awareness of the deep connections of all things. These experiences forever change our perspective and our relationship to life.

Our ability to access more refined levels of awareness can be developed when we understand that each of us actually possesses a number of bodies, as depicted in the graphic above. At our densest level, we have a physical body, which we experience with our physical senses. It is sometimes called the third-dimensional body, because the physical world is three-dimensional. (The print in a book or a TV picture is two-dimensional.)

Our next level, the mental/emotional body, exists within and slightly beyond the physical body at a higher vibrational rate. This is where we experience thoughts and feelings. Both the conscious and unconscious aspects of the mind dwell here. This fourth-dimensional body is not visible to most people, but still expresses duality (good/bad, dark/light, etc.).

Vibrating at even higher rates are the spiritual levels of consciousness, from our individual souls on up to Infinite Intelligence–the fifth dimension and above. As we become more aware of who we are at these higher levels, a conscious connection with Spirit takes place. We have the opportunity to integrate the power of that awareness into our physical world. When the awareness of our Oneness is real, we cannot help but interact differently with others. As we are changed, the world around us appears very different.

Breath is the most crucial and dynamic tool we can use to master our consciousness. Neither angels nor gurus can save us from ourselves or make us into conscious beings. Life is a do-it-yourself endeavor. There are no two ways about it: We entered human form to expand our potential as spiritual beings by learning to master life here, to bridge the gap between human personality and higher consciousness. We use the tool of breath to unite all of our bodies in order to achieve harmony and balance in our every-day world.

The breath is a tangible vehicle through which spiritual energy manifests in the physical universe. Spiritual energy can also be considered the primordial Life Force, the divine energy that bestows the miraculous gift of life. It is intimately connected with the breathing process in that the more breath we can take in, the more filled with this force we become.

Andrew Weil, MD., exclaims in his popular audio series on breathing, "The breath is the movement of Spirit in the body."

Transformational Breathing is the art and science of fully integrating our spirit body with our physical body, and helping restore the natural connection among body, mind, and spirit. It allows us to go beyond the levels of body and mind to encounter the transpersonal.

By using Transformational Breathing, we raise the vibrational frequency of our electromagnetic field, becoming energetically lighter or more enlightened. We elevate our frequency to such a rate that we become fully identified with our Spiritual Self or Soul. Enlightenment brings us to a state of bliss and enables us to experience the ecstatic and transcendent realms.

But this awareness alone does not solve our worldly prob-lems. Action must follow insight as we learn to walk our talk. Problems do not always disappear, but we learn to welcome and surf each incoming wave. When we live this way, every so-called problem is perceived as an opportunity to redefine and expand our sense of aliveness, our sense of joy. And so it is.

*"Joy is a vibration.
It can be experienced as
laughter, movement,
peace and clarity of mind,
and abundant physicall well-being.*

Vywamus

Part Two

*"Blending conscious and unconscious
wisdom has always marked the genius
in the world of scientific discovery...
Newton, Einstein, Watson and Crick.
The genius of Transformational Breathing
is the blending of the conscious and unconscious
mind, within each one of us, to discover
how to achieve our highest potential."*

Christopher C. French, M.D.,
Shelburne Falls, MA

11

Breathing into
Love, Power and Joy

The three licks of flame at the center of the Transformational Breathing Foundation's logo represent those three expressions that seem to emerge and prevail again and again in this work: love, power, and joy. In fact, for those who practice the breathing, these words come to be seen as synonymous with Transformational Breathing.

Ironically, love, power, and joy are humankind's three most hunted treasures, yet most people have never fully experienced them in the truest sense. Love is often experienced as self-sacrificing, jealous, needy, wanton, painful, exclusive, limited, fragile, conditional, or manipulative. Power is frequently felt as a temporary rush or state of satisfaction after influencing someone else's beliefs or actions. And joy is regarded as pie-in-the-sky fantasy—something that doesn't really exist for more than a few minutes after an orgasm or a drug-induced high.

Let's talk about love. Love is the most powerful force in the universe. More than anything else, I hear people say that Transformational Breathing is the most loving work they have ever experienced. It extends the love of the Creator/Source to everyone involved in a session. It is the breath that ignites Divine Love within each heart.

This is very different from the typical, day-to-day form of love with which we are most familiar – "I love you as long as you do or give me what I want." Often love cannot truly be enjoyed because of the common beliefs that "All good things must come to an end," and "Love hurts." These ideas are lived out as simple fact in many people's reality. Authentic love never requires coercion, disempowerment, or self-abuse. Instead, it nurtures our growth and allows us to become our truest, fullest selves.

Unconditional love is the healing force of the universe, yet few of us have ever truly experienced it. Most of us have been loved by other personalities who wanted to get something from us. Unconditional love just *is*. It expects nothing from us, accepts us just the way we are, and sees us as *inherently perfect*. This understanding is something that grows in the consciousness of those trained in and practicing Transformational Breathing. It is part of the spiritual expansion that occurs naturally as a result of reaching expanded states of consciousness within each breathing session.

The gap between conditional and unconditional love is not small. In fact, it looms as large as the Grand Canyon! We can reduce or eliminate that chasm with Transformational Breathing, giving us an experience of the Love that moves mountains and shakes worlds.

Let's talk about power. If the word turns you off, chances are you believe it's dangerous, or perhaps you don't believe you have much of it. Others may seem to overpower you. If the word "power" brings a wanton feeling and slight flutter to your gut, you may not believe you have enough, and often try, unconsciously, to take it from others. On the other hand, if your reaction to the concept of power is a relaxed, alive, joyful sense of well-being and strength, you are probably a conscious breather.

Power itself is neither good nor bad. Like fire, it can either keep us toasty warm or destroy an entire forest. How we acquire power and what we do with it determine its role in our lives. This depends entirely on where we focus our attention and intention. On a deeper, more personal level, the way we perceive the origin and availability of power determines our own happiness. If we constantly focus our attention and intention on trying to *gain* power, we will always feel a need to create *more* power.

There are two kinds of personal power. One is false and one is real. One is fear and one is love. Using manipulation and fear tactics, we can aim to take from others and claim it for ourselves. In his book, *The Celestine Prophecy*, James Redfield developed a very good working model of this concept. His "control dramas" well describe how we literally drain energy from each other using behavior patterns that seduce others into engaging in our agenda instead of their own. This form of power is based on weakness, however. Not unlike raping the earth or waging war in the quest for power, fear-based power is easily depleted, leading to more manipulation and destruction.

Real power is based on love and creativity. We find it naturally when we open ourselves to the life around us; an abundance of higher power that beckons daily simply to be received. It is easily replenished and leads to more love and creativity—like the sun, which freely gives us its power, warmth, and light.

Advertisers tell us that fresh breath brings power—the power to win love from a beautiful person, or excel at that next job interview. The truth is that neither love nor power comes from the sweet-smelling breath you get with a mouthwash. Contrary to popular belief, real power does not come from *anything* outside of you. In fact, the real irony here is that if we were a society of conscious breathers, we would naturally need and want much less, because we would know we already have it! We would know that unlimited power flows freely from within.

However, if we continue to honor the validity of what is going on outside of us more than we honor what is going on inside ourselves, then we hold ourselves captive to chaos. If I am paying more attention to others' truths, how can I possibly discover or express my own? How can I ever find out who I really am? Unfortunately, many of us chase myriad images of random realities instead of focusing on creating our own. We get deeply involved in soap operas, wrestling matches, political dramas, community gossip, sports legends, movies, and so forth. Many of us know more about the TV characters than we know about ourselves! I am not saying these things are bad. I *am* asking you to look at your own life at least as closely. It is the medium that you have been given to access true power to express and create your Self.

Every time we take a breath, we are taking in power. The deeper our breath, the more deeply our power is anchored, and the more energy we have at our disposal. There are many names for such power. Einstein called it *energy*. Yogis call it *life force*, or, in Sanskrit, *prana*. Asian cultures call it *chi* or *ki*. Western scientists call it *oxygen*. In the Aramaic Bible, Jesus calls it the *Angel of Air*.

The Latin word for breath is *spiritus,* and our breath (our re*spir*ation) is how we receive the power of *Spir*it. It is also how we receive in*spir*ation and how we a*spir*e to greater heights. With Transformational Breathing, we quickly come to realize the authenticity of our spiritual self, and to freely and fully express Spirit. That is the ultimate power of the universe.

Let's talk about joy. Everyone wants it, but some have no clue what it is, or how it feels. Some even fear because their reality feels threatened without dramatic problems. What if I wasn't heartbroken about my last failed relationship? What if losing my job was no big deal? What if I didn't spend every minute worrying about our children, our parents, our friends, our pets, our bills, our cars? What would I do? This is where fear creeps in and justifies the postponement of joy.

The yogi master Vywamus says it best: "Joy is an energy which, when activated, allows you to simply BE… relaxed and accessible to the other transforming energies that you have invoked in seeking to know yourself. When you breathe, you ignite the subtle vibration of joy that can be experienced within the physical and emotional bodies. Joy has never been lost to you… You have decided it will not be felt. Let the joy build in your bodies as you breathe. Joy doesn't seek to draw anything from anyone else, or seek to manipulate another. It is whole within itself. It is self-promoting, self-creating. What it will do is to radiate outward and simply touch others."

Can you imagine feeling whole and joyous most of the time? How would it feel to be trusting and satisfied with whatever arises in your day-to-day experience? These are feelings that thousands of people report as a result of Transformational Breathing. With a commitment to regular breathing sessions, this transformation to a life of love, power, and joy is inevitable and surprisingly rapid.

12

Sex and Intimacy in Relationships

In the neo-Christian discourse, *A Course In Miracles*, Jesus tells us there are only two kinds of relationships: holy relationships and those of the ego. The holy relationship is when two or more whole beings come together and reflect their wholeness to each other. They join for the purposes of knowing and communing with God.

Ego relationships, on the other hand, are based on need. When we are looking for our "other half," we are trying to get something from someone else. The problem with this is that what we really want can only be found inside of ourselves as the divine or sacred. Most ego relationships are doomed to fail, because outer focus pulls us out of our inward journey, where truth and Self are found. Transformational Breathing can bring our focus back to our inner oneness and allows for the possibility of holy relationship with another.

Today, the idea of intimacy has become synonymous with sexual relations. But not all sexual relationships are intimate, and not all intimate relationships are sexual. When sex and intimacy do come together, we experience a delicious remembrance of our essential oneness with others.

Perhaps this is the very reason we simultaneously long for and dread the experience of deep intimacy. Intimacy is a deep sense of connectedness with another. It represents the end of resistance to knowing that they are a part of you and you are a part of them. We desire the experience of oneness, yet we fear losing our individuality.

At our deepest level, we are all absolutely connected always. Our longing for intimacy in relationships is the longing to experience through the mind and physical body what we already are at the level of soul. Our souls are just waiting for our bodies to feel more, to experience more and to recreate ourselves in the duality that makes up this three-dimensional world.

Returning to the awareness of our soul connection typically involves a tenuous attempt to allow intimate expression through the mind and the body. It sometimes begins as an exploration of the possibilities of compatibility on the intellectual level, deciding whether we have enough interests and values in common to go further into intimacy. Next we may begin to share emotional aspects of the mind. And at some point, that quest for intimacy may be expressed through physical affection and/or sexual relationship.

In order to feel safe and accepted by another, we take gradually-increasing levels of risk, testing the waters and discovering solid ground for a relationship. Risking means we have to allow ourselves to be vulnerable—to show our weaknesses, fears, and deepest desires.

We often equate vulnerability with being weak, but allowing ourselves to express our vulnerability is key to self-acceptance and overcoming fear of intimacy. When we experience our true nature as Spirit, we begin to see vulnerability as an opportunity to reconnect with the whole. The famous quote from Scripture, "Whenever two or more are gathered in my name, there I shall be," comes to mind as a well-documented way to confirm what occurs when we willingly invite another human being to permeate our personal walls of protection.

Transformational Breathing brings us fully into the awareness and experience of our True Nature, engulfed in God's unconditional Love. From this perspective of ultimate truth, absolute safety and love are experienced from within. We no longer need to strive to *create* intimacy with others, because our internal experience naturally extends outward as the experience of being truly safe and loving with a partner. The self-judgment that once led to inhibition dissolves, and the capacity for intimacy blossoms.

Allowing ourselves to be vulnerable and tender is effortless when we are accepting ourselves and not seeking that acceptance elsewhere. By connecting us with our inner truth, full, connected breathing opens us to the reality that there is nothing to defend. This understanding leads to the deep intimacy that we all crave.

In addition to facilitating our inner journey, conscious deep breathing in unison with another creates a sense of deep connection. This can be experienced as an incredibly intimate and nonsexual communion between friends. Breathing together while making love is even more profound. The literal blending of bodies, minds, and souls can take us beyond climactic states and into oneness.

The more deeply we breathe during a sexual interlude, the more we can relax and enjoy, give and receive, and ultimately experience complete communion. This also intensifies the senses – both physically and emotionally. When the body armor is relaxed and emotional walls are down, the mere touch of another can bring ecstasy. It only requires our intentional focus on that which unifies our souls: the breath.

 Relaxing our body and mind allows us to receive and enjoy our lover's touch so much more that the climactic experience reaches new heights. Breathing moves energy throughout the body, and with conscious intention and relaxed focus, orgasm can become more readily available and all-encompassing.

Henry and Dr. Janet Leslie Orion are facilitators and trainers of the Transformational Breathing training program in Asheville, North Carolina. Together they have discovered that fully connected breathing during sex "increases the pleasure and joy of our lovemaking and enables us to experience what we call 'spiritual intercourse.'" Henry agreed to share with us this particularly memorable experience.

Being in nature under the stars and moon and breathing together enhanced our energy and aliveness during a very long evening of enjoyable lovemaking. At the point when I was reaching orgasm, my breathing intensi- fied tremendously and I felt a strong urge to rise up on my knees. My head tilted up and back opening my throat to the power of the breath that was flowing intensely in and out of me. Each inhalation felt like all the energy of the universe was entering my body. Each exhalation seemed to leave me from the core of my being and extend to the outer reaches of the heavens. My breathing continued to intensify and I felt that my entire body was opening up to the Great Spirit. My arms raised up in an open gesture to the sky. Time disappeared and I am not sure how long I continued the fully activated, powerful breathing.

I then stopped breathing and there was total silence, stillness, and an extraordinary light. I do not remember hearing the sounds of the summer forest. I was in another incredibly expanded dimension of myself. It was absolute bliss. Suddenly, my breathing reactivated. With one powerfully long inhalation, I physically rose up again with my arms extended to the heavens as I continued breathing in a full connected rhythm. With each inhalation, I felt the energy of the cosmos descend through my body into Janet. She felt like Mother Earth to me as she held my thighs and waist, connecting deeply with me physically. Through her, all this positive energy from the universe descended into the earth.

I was physically and spiritually connected with Janet, and together we were the Alpha and Omega conduit for the interchange of powerful energy between the heavens and the earth. This interlude continued for quite some time. As my muscles, bones and essence filled with this energy, I became totally aware of the absolute interconnectedness of everything. There is no separation. We are All One.

As we commune with others with the intention of knowing and honoring Source, we discover a common bond of higher purpose. This allows the flow of energy to shift from a horizontal flow to a vertical one. Instead of looking outward to and from each other for completion, we focus our attention and intention upward to that higher level of awareness. The reason for being together is no longer personality exchange. It becomes a relationship with God that is expressed through each other.

Many conscious breathers are reporting experiences of the holy relationship, where there is no competition or need, only a mutual quest for what is eternal and true. These relationships are fulfilling because they are founded on that which is eternal. Within such union we find mutual growth and support. We share in honoring of the sacredness of life and our relationship to the Divine. And beyond even the experience of divine intimate relationship, the power of our breath ultimately brings us full circle to the only true relationship that exists: Our relationship with ourselves, perfect and whole, reflected in everyone and everything that we see.

"The breathing helped me tremendously during my pregnancy. Giving birth to twins certainly had its challenges, but I breathed through them, and continue to do so with the challenges of parenting."

Joni Foster-Robison

13

The Art of Giving Birth

Since procreation is our highest creative act, it holds the most tremendous potential for expressing our Life Force energy. When a child is conceived, it is the result of a primal expression of two complementary forces of life—yin and yang, masculine and feminine, man and woman. From this union of duality grows a unique new expression of love, a fresh new vehicle for the embodiment of spirit.

Contrary to popular belief, an infant is not a small being. Composed of perhaps fifteen percent physical body and eighty-five percent Spirit or Life Force, a newborn fills the room with the pure energy of consciousness. The potential for creation is at its all time high since *our* consciousness blends in and "pours" into their bodies. The physical body grows before our eyes, drawing from that original eighty-five percent—the electromagnetic field of Life Force energy, which is also pure awareness.

Without our own awareness and conscious appreciation of this profound opportunity for creative expression, however, potential often goes unrealized. If Leonardo da Vinci had been limited to one paintbrush and two colors, for example, how much of his creative power might we all have missed? Color and stroke were expressions of his Life Force as he gave life to paint and canvas. Together, these elements took on a life of their own. The true value of his art comes from its effect on peoples' lives.

Only when we fully appreciate and embrace the power of our own Life Force will we recognize our full creative potential and embrace procreation as the sacred form of art that it is. Would any of us willingly place a work by da Vinci on a graffiti-covered wall in an inner city war zone? Only when parents begin to see the entire process of reproduction as their own sacred form of artistic creation will there be more peace on earth. Of course, an infant is not a blank canvas. Quite the contrary. Each child is born with a unique design and the God-given talents and predispositions to fulfill a unique purpose. Like any good artist, however, parents must prepare, support, and release their children, as soon as they are ready, to a valued life of their own.

It is our responsibility and privilege to provide as much vibrant color and as many creative tools on the palette as possible. We do this by passing on an abundance of Life Force. Like the oxygen mask on an airplane, we must first give it to ourselves and then make sure our children get plenty.

A blockage of essential Life Force can actually prevent the conception of a child. Infertility is often a matter of repressed energy flow to our reproductive organs, our creative center.

Over the years, I have coached numerous women who had been unsuccessful at becoming pregnant. We found better breathing to be the key. I first became aware of the possibility with a woman who was drawn to me for breathwork because of another issue entirely. After several sessions, though, she found herself blissfully pregnant in a marriage that had greatly improved over the course of her breath therapy. Since then, word has spread and now it is fairly common for people to come to the breath motivated by the desire to conceive a child.

Joni Foster-Robison had been trying to get pregnant when she began taking our facilitator training with the goal of enhancing her healing practice and thus her own healing.

"I look back on my second and third breathing sessions and remember the extreme cramping in my lower abdomen." Joni recalls. "It was very distracting, but I did my best to breathe into it. After the third session I didn't feel it again. What a relief! The very next month, we got pregnant—and not with just one baby, but two!"

"It was during the in-water breathing session that I first realized and experienced the joy of being pregnant. I can't help but wonder if the energy blocks I released in my abdomen might have otherwise inhibited us from conceiving for much longer. I truly believe that Transformational Breathing is what welcomed our two little spirits into our life. It's a miracle I will never forget and give thanks for every day."

I do believe that a lot of infertility problems are due to inadequate abdominal breathing (preventing oxygenation) and thus held emotions (energy without flow). A miracle can be but a breath session away.

It has been incredibly rewarding to hear about all the little "breath babies" who have arrived since the addition of Joni's twin boys.

Another exciting aspect of this work is breathing with pregnant women and their families. Transformational Breathing holds the potential to revolutionize the birth process, not only directly, in that it makes labor and delivery more joyful and less painful for baby and mother, but also indirectly by healing the existing birth trauma of the parents. In fully healing and integrating the birth ordeal, it also clears the path toward deep spiritual bonding between parents and children.

Joni, mother of the "breath twins" was thrilled. "The breathing helped me tremendously during my pregnancy. It helped me to be fully present with Isaac and Tristan, to listen and support their [in-utero] process. Giving birth to twins certainly had its challenges, but I breathed through them, and continue to do so with the challenges of parenting."

When a mother-to-be commits to healing her own life and breath, it will impact the lives of many. She will be more able to enjoy giving birth, and the infant will receive more of what he needs in the process. It will prepare her for the challenges of responsible parenting, and she'll even be better prepared to maintain a loving relationship with the child's father.

And after witnessing the positive changes in mom, dad is likely to begin his own transformational journey (if he has not done so already). Other children in the family will also reap the benefits of more capable and loving parents. And last but not least, a breath session for the newborn cleans the slate, allowing a vibrant new expression of Life Force to blossom from seeds of unconditional love. The potential for a happy, healthy family is once again increased exponentially.

Most people are totally unaware of how traumatic the birth process can be. There seems to be widespread misconception of the awareness level of the newborn, who is generally considered unable to feel or perceive much. This misconception is not really so surprising, though, since we don't usually remember what happened to us. Our own early traumatic memories have been repressed into the deepest hidden layers of the subconscious mind. Therefore, we assume that infants are just not aware.

Yet there is a great deal of evidence supporting the fact that newborns are quite conscious and tremendously aware, despite the developing state of their brain and nervous system. In addition to the scientific evidence, this awareness has been confirmed by many thousands of people who have reexperienced their birth during a conscious breathing session.

As a matter of fact, infants tend to be far *more* sensitive to external thoughts and stimuli than most adults. After all, they are mostly pure consciousness. Unfortunately, their heightened sensitivities are denied in the modern physical birth experience. Many delivery practices border on brutal and can leave major scars on the most basic foundation of a child's mind.

I've heard people say things like, "Oh, children are so resilient. They always bounce back." I seldom hear this from conscious breathers, however, who have overcome the need to deny and repress their own historical pain. Our society's need for this information is tremendous, especially now, when some children are "bouncing back" from repressed pain with guns and bombs aimed at each other in our schools!

Knowing that the newcomer is fully aware and paying close attention, sometimes from the very moment of conception, gives us the impetus to be as sensitive as possible to everything that occurs during pregnancy. It is important and quite possible to create a more positive and loving *in utero* experience. The mother and father must not only take care of their physical bodies, but also be aware of emotional input and expression.

During pregnancy, it is important to be as loving, kind, and nurturing as possible to themselves and to the baby. It is also helpful to talk to the unborn child, expressing how pleased and excited they are that he is coming and how much they love him.

And when the time of birth arrives, we can ease the transition for our babies by helping them feel more welcomed and respected. We can bring more awareness and gentleness into the birthing room by informing doctors, midwives, childbirth educators, parents, and others, of the potential for trauma. We can even show them how to heal their own trauma through breath sessions. The bottom line is that we have the technology to transform the frightening ordeal of birth into a trusted and celebrated event. And it's time that we do.

During birth itself, we can give our child a positive experience. The first step is to recognize that children fully experience and feel the journey down the birth canal, a journey incredibly stimulating and different from anything they have experienced up to that point. This is the first time they feel any pressure on their bodies—over forty pounds per square inch! Scientists believe this experience initializes certain brain activity. The fresh new skin feels it all; the subconscious mind records it all; and the entering spirit notices every nuance of feeling in the room. Everything that is going on during labor, right down to the mother's state of mind, is the newcomer's first glimpse of life in a body.

One very beneficial thing that can be done during labor is to positively frame our emotional experience of the contractions. Instead of fearing and resisting "labor pains," dreading each contraction, and practicing pain management breathing techniques just to get through it, we can use conscious breathing to breathe deeply into the experience and begin to perceive each contraction as an opportunity to relax and surrender to the power of creation. With the inner knowing and faith that comes from the practice of Transformational Breathing, this is much easier than it sounds.

Transformational Breathing techniques have been used very effectively during labor to integrate the intensity of contractions. For a variety of compelling reasons, it is a far more comprehensive tool than the commonly used Lamaze method of breathing.

Lamaze breathing can cause hyperventilation due to the strong, forceful style of exhalation. This blowing technique creates an imbalance in the carbon dioxide to oxygen ratio, which produces an alkaloid state that is medically undesirable. While it does help to take the focus off the pain of contractions, it does nothing to aid the process of birth itself.

Forced exhalation during birth creates a tightening of the muscles in the solar plexus and abdomen, which prevents the breath and energy from flowing freely throughout the system. Lamaze breathing does not promote the relaxation essential for the smooth flow of Life Force energy, which is so strong during contractions. It actually causes resistance to this energy and thereby intensifies the experience of tension during labor.

In Transformational Breathing, our attention is focused on drawing in the breath. This provides the additional supply of oxygen necessary for strenuous activity. And by fully relaxing as we exhale, we prevent hyperventilation or alkalosis, and we unblock the energy flow so it can move more freely in the process. The only immediate side effects are that it relaxes the mind and body, welcomes the Life Force energy, and supplies the increased oxygen demands of both mother and baby.

Once surrender, based on faith, replaces resistance, based on fear, pain is reduced and can actually transform into pleasure. In fact, it is not unheard of for very relaxed and in-tune mothers to experience sensations akin to orgasm while giving birth.

Simply addressing the above concerns will benefit mom and baby tremendously. It is also necessary to remember that the infant is new to this world and needs to be treated with the utmost of thoughtful kindness. The newborn babe is extremely sensitive to light and sound, since up to this point, the dark warmth and muffled quiet of mommy's womb has been home. Soft, gentle lighting in the delivery room is far preferable to shocking the baby with the brightness of spotlights.

It is important to be aware of what is being said and the volume and tone at which it is spoken. Words, and even unspoken thoughts, will be stored in the infant's hungry subconscious mind, influencing every single experience from that moment forward. Loud, obtrusive noise is an assault on the baby's tiny ears and tender nervous system. Soft music and quietly spoken praises of the child's beauty and magnificence are beneficial, along with affirmation of how happy and excited everyone is that baby has arrived.

Another common hospital practice is putting drops of silver nitrate in the infant's eyes to prevent infection in case the mother has a venereal disease. What most people do not realize is that those drops cause burning pain and temporary blindness for the infant. Wouldn't it just be kinder to do a simple test on the mother for the disease?

Today, childbirth is classified by many hospitals and medical professionals as a medical emergency. This is a sad statement about our society. Yet the real irony lies in the way the infant is treated! Any other surgical procedure would include far more consideration of the patient's comfort.

Let's put ourselves, for a moment, in the baby's booties. It is important to be vigilant in remembering that everything the child feels—and the child *does* feel and remember everything—is amplified because of the newness. This information comes from thousands of clients and trainees who have reported vivid and verifiable memories of being born.

For example, forceps can place excruciating pressure on tender temples, causing great pain, trauma and sometimes, physical disabilities. The need to pull the baby out can frequently be avoided by, again, surrendering to and cooperating with the natural ingenious process of birth, and by not making time and money a priority.

One breath facilitator, Lois C., described the six-hour delivery of her only child, Angela, as "amazingly enjoyable except for the forty-five minutes of pushing. With each breath, I was able to smile and consciously relax my cervix. I could actually feel myself opening up in more ways than one. And I could feel the sense of oneness with my baby as we moved through the experience together. It was the most precious and empowering experience of my life, and I know it would not have been experienced in this way had I not surrendered to the Life Force through my breathing."

Midwives have long understood that there is a direct physiological connection between the jaw and the pelvis. More specifically, when we relax the jaw as we exhale, the pelvic floor softens simultaneously. A mother of five boys and a professional midwife for twenty-three years, Sushila Schwerin from Lenox, Massachusetts, recites the age-old wisdom of midwifery, "A loose, open mouth and open throat make for a loose open cervix."

She also adds, "Toning and sounding are also excellent for channeling the energy of birth in a positive way. It causes opening instead of restriction and is conducive to going with the birth force instead of resisting it. A round mouth with deliberate open primal sounds is beneficial, whereas the more typical screaming or screeching out in reaction to pain is the result of closing the throat and resisting the force of nature. Instead of the energy being bottled up inside, it can be released in a way that makes the muscles more functional." Consider, as an example, the primal sounds often made by weight lifters as they push the weight off their chests.

Sushila is quick to clarify however that "during the pushing phase of childbirth, it is more beneficial to close the throat to harness the energy and support the downward force."

Having a strong abdominal diaphragm is helpful here as well, another benefit of practicing full diaphragmatic breathing.

If the infant emerges with the umbilical cord wrapped around the neck, we could affirm that it is easy and safe to breathe, while unwrapping it, and that everything is okay—as opposed to increasing the trauma by panicking. Unless it's wrapped very tight, chances are the infant is still getting oxygen from the womb through the umbilical cord.

Another very important way to ease the trauma is by not cutting the cord too soon. We need to give the newborn time to acclimate to a new way of receiving oxygen, and to allow the lungs those precious moments to open according to the laws of nature. In the animal kingdom, a gradual transition from mother's oxygen supply to breathing independently is common, as the umbilical cord continues to pulse, supplying oxygen to the newborn for up to an hour. Before the days of hospital deliveries, this natural process was more common for humankind as well.

"When little Angela was laid upon my chest, umbilical cord still attached," remembers Lois, "her tiny head popped up to meet my eyes for our first hello. Her twinkling eyes held mine for several seconds. It seemed like an eternity, and then she smiled and rested her cheek on my breast. All the nurses were amazed, since newborns usually cannot lift their heads for several days or more."

This transition period allows the young one to adapt to temperature, light intensity, first touch to the skin, the excitement in the room, the first thrilling glance into mommy and daddy's adoring eyes. It also allows any remnants of the fluid that has filled the lungs for nine months, to dissipate naturally instead of being sucked out forcefully.

Lois recalls, "Angela's first sobbing tears came when a nurse suddenly began shoving a syringe down her throat to suck out mucus. I stopped her, angrily, but the damage was done. I was very upset about this. In a later breath session, I remembered and resolved trauma from a mucus syringe at my own birth. It was an unwelcome invasion and it hurt physically too! I realized in that session that years and years of recurring strep throat had its origins in that incident. I no longer suffer from strep, though Angela does."

Are we arrogant or faithless enough to assume that the Creator failed to plan for one of our most important transitions? If so, it is time to regain faith by experiencing the awesome perfection of God's love in a breathing session. Again, it is a matter of trusting and surrendering to the laws of nature. Joy and harmony are part of the Divine Plan. When we resist the natural birth process and plan things according to our own artificial needs, we cause ourselves, and our children, pain and trouble.

Honoring and allowing the natural process ensures that baby's first breath of life is not accompanied by desperate feelings of fear and panic, similar to the common anxiety attacks with which so many people suffer today. The sensation of suffocation resulting from the lack of oxygen leads to an initial struggle for life, which can follow the child throughout every aspect of their life. If the cord is allowed to remain intact until no longer needed, safety and comfort will be associated with that initial breath, and, from the very beginning, your child will establish a healthy acceptance of Life Force.

Unless there are emergency circumstances, the child should not be separated from her parents. Many babies are whisked away to the nursery just moments after birth and placed in little plastic tubs with no one to cuddle or comfort them. This is simply traditional hospital practice. There is no good reason for it.

Natural childbirth programs allowing same-room labor, delivery and recovery are becoming more and more popular, but tradition still reigns. It is essential that the child remain with the parents immediately after birth for as long as possible. Holding, snuggling, and nursing the baby ease the transition into this world and allow her to feel safe and cherished in her new environment. Unless sedated with drugs, a tired mother can safely sleep with her baby, knowing that mothers' instinct will not allow her to roll over on her child.

After being whisked from mother's arms, most boys are then circumcised, adding one more intensely traumatic surgical procedure to the long list of assaults endured in the very first day of breathing in a body. Although it is considered normal in this "civilized" society, to have the most sensitive part of the most cherished organ removed, there is no valid evidence left to support health reasons once used to justify this assault—in fact evidence now shows it is healthier to leave foreskin intact. And the damage to the psyche is known by many conscious breathers to far outweigh the perceived importance of fitting in to current norms or outdated health concerns. Nevertheless, men and women continue to deny that the child feels, or is affected by, the pain and anguish.

Rick, a man in his mid-forties, came to understand and began to resolve a long-standing resentment toward his mother, which he never quite could explain. In a breath session he vividly recalls his own circumcision:

"I was so angry with her. How could she betray me like this? How could she let them do this to me? I didn't understand what was going on, all I knew was the searing pain and the feeling of being attacked and not protected. This anger toward my mother persisted throughout my whole life, until I did a breath session and saw it in a different light. My mother never meant to hurt me. She thought she was doing what was right."

Innovative Childbirth Program

After discovering the power of Transformational Breathing, Judith Taché left her career of more than twenty-five years in traditional nursing to begin sharing what she had learned of holistic approaches to health and well-being. Since 1994, her private practice has been providing personal transformational services throughout New England and Texas. Most recently, she has been focusing her efforts on working with pregnant women to ease and enrich their pregnancy, delivery and parenting experiences.

Judy is a Certified Transformational Breathing Facilitator, Reiki Master, Registered Nurse and is trained in hospice care. As an RN, she has worked in rehabilitative, pediatric, pre- and postpartum nursing and in special care nurseries. She is also experienced in Polarity Therapy and Cranio-Sacral therapy.

As early in the pregnancy as possible, Judy encourages mothers and partners to come to a two-hour workshop called *Nurturing Your Unborn Child.* This evening session includes an introduction to Transformational Breathing, sharing about fears or concerns, and visualizing the birth setting. This whole process can vary somewhat, from one session to the next, according to the unique issues presented by participants.

A psychologist who attended Judy's program reported: "I felt like myself—strong, healthy, and confident—for the first time in approximately two months since the pregnancy began. This was a wonderful oasis after days and days of vomiting and feeling tired. During the breathing exercises I was free of feeling ill and instead felt full of love for my baby."

Judy adds, "The physicians at the office where I am working are supporting the program more as they get positive feedback from patients regarding their stress levels, fear reduction, and that wonderful sense of deepening peace."

Christiane Northrup, M.D., author of *Women's Bodies, Women's Wisdom*, who enjoys Transformational Breathing, has also come to appreciate the program for pregnant women. She says, "I have personally benefited from the gifts Judy brings to breathwork, and I would highly recommend the course for pregnant women."

Judy sees mothers making a much clearer sense of connection with the baby and their own inner self. If partners come, they share in the experience.

Judy says, "There is a sacredness that the parents are able to step into in regard to their relationship to the pregnancy and the baby."

According to M.L.B., a participant in the class, "I went to five sessions and each experience was unique in its own way. I had my first session when I was six months pregnant. In the Transformational Breathing part, I felt sensations I had never experienced before. It was a little scary at first, but I do remember feeling very safe, relaxed and calm. In the guided imagery part, I actually visualized my child. I saw that it was a boy. I was overcome with a feeling I had never ever felt before. When explaining that feeling to a few of my friends, most said the same thing—it's the feeling of unconditional love for your child! What an incredible, awesome, overwhelming feeling of joy and love! I left the first session feeling very clear."

As a result of the breathing sessions, mothers seem much more able to let go of any fearful energy coming at them from family, co-workers, and friends, rather than taking it on as another stress factor. It seems very common for pregnant women to receive advice from many sources, and this self-empowerment process enables them to more easily pick and choose what serves them. As the fears subside, love and trust begin to open more and more fully. It is as if the baby becomes more a partner in the pregnancy rather than just the object of it.

Judy also reports specific advantages during delivery itself for women who practice Transformational Breathing. During labor, their breathing naturally flows into the Transformational Breathing, even though they may have had classes in the Lamaze method. Judy says, "It's clear to me that as the abdomen opens more and more fully it becomes progressively easier for the mother to enter into the contraction phase of the delivery process, rather than attempting to stay separate from it by breathing only into the upper body. This seems to transform the entire process from one of avoidance to one of merging with, and embracing, the experience."

In addition, a far less complicated postpartum period is common. Mothers report a very deep sense of connection with baby. Babies seem to adjust more easily after delivery and beyond. In general, there is a more flowing transition from one phase to the next. She adds, "The mother's relationship with extended family also tends to go through a process of improvement and transformation as the mother embodies a truer sense of her empowered self."

Another participant offered, "It is amazing how, through directed breathing, I have been able not only to release many of my negative feelings, but also to make a connection with my child to the point where we actually communicate with one another during the sessions. I intend to continue with these relaxation exercises well after the baby is born, because it is a perfect way to temporarily extract myself from life's everyday stresses and at the same time focus on self-improvement as well as self-fulfillment."

Carol's Experience

Carol, a thirty-year-old mother of two, used Transformational Breathing extensively with her third pregnancy. During her first pregnancy, at the age of eighteen, she'd had very little support or information on what to do and what to expect. The delivery of her first child was a hospital nightmare. During a long labor, she was full of fear, pain and, ultimately, drugs. And, after all her efforts, she felt forced to give the baby up for adoption, because of her age and circumstances.

The second pregnancy and labor were somewhat better, since Carol knew more about what to expect. This time she chose to birth at home and used Lamaze breathing, which was helpful during early labor, but proved ineffective during hard labor. After ten hours of intense labor, she gave birth to her second child, a son.

Shortly after his birth, Carol learned about Transformational Breathing and began practicing it. She felt its immediate effects on her stress levels and her ability to stay centered and calm, even in the worst moments of raising a small, active child. Before long,

Carol felt drawn to the Facilitator Training, and began sharing it with others in her community. When she discovered that she was pregnant for the third time, she knew that it would be a valuable tool during the pregnancy and delivery.

Says Carol, "During labor, my partner, who had also graduated the facilitator training, coached me with the Transformational Breathing during the contractions. This made them much easier to handle and some were even enjoyable. The labor went quickly and before long it was time to push. I knew that since it was my third child, things would be easier. But I could also feel how much the breathing integrated the energy of each contraction to the point that I could cooperate with the labor process rather than resist it. My midwife said it was one of the smoothest deliveries she had ever attended. She later said she was interested in learning more about using Transformational Breathing in her work."

The Birth of Caleb

At the time of this writing, it has been four years since the birth of my second grandchild, Caleb Hunter. His mother, my daughter Rebecca, was eighteen years old at the time and was somewhat apprehensive about giving birth. She had attended a few prenatal classes and was beginning to get some idea of what to expect. Being the fourth of eight children, she also had been closely connected to the birth of her younger siblings. Two of those births had been at home, and although she was young, Rebecca had been there. Since the onset of her own unexpected pregnancy, she had used Transformational Breathing to help integrate the emotions that arose.

Her official labor began about five o'clock one Thursday morning. By eleven, the contractions were strong enough to bring her to tears. They were still fifteen minutes apart so there was no rush to get to the hospital. She instinctively started doing the Transformational Breath with each contraction. Her ability to handle the contractions improved with the breathing, even though they were getting more intense. Soon they were ten minutes apart. By the time we got to the hospital, Rebecca was in full labor. Each time she felt a contraction build, she began to do the connected breathing, which helped her relax and dissipate the pain.

Her labor progressed very well, and by five-in the afternoon she had gone through transition and was ready to push. Toward the end, when Rebecca began requesting medication, we encouraged her to hang in there and keep breathing, which she did. That was enough to help her complete the delivery without drugs—much healthier for mother and child.

This was a short labor for a first-time birth. The pushing stage went rapidly as well, and at 5:28 that evening, Caleb was born at eight pounds, four ounces. Later Rebecca said the breathing kept her focused and helped her make it through each contraction without losing control. "Even the nurses thought I did a great job, and I know the breathing helped."

Water Birthing

Many women are now choosing to birth their babies in warm water, allowing the infant to swim around awhile before coming into the much cooler room temperature environment. The baby comes from a fluid environment, which makes water a perfect transitional element. These babies are generally known to be far more peaceful and alert than usual. If this type of delivery is not preferable or practical, a warm, soothing bath for mommy during labor and for baby soon after birth can ease and calm mom and baby tremendously.

According to Molly Connelly, a professional midwife for over twenty-five years and Executive Director of the New Hampshire Childbirth Educators Association, "Breathing is central to opening up to the birthing experience." After treating herself and her colleagues to private and group breathing sessions, respectively, she arranged a private session with me for her daughter. Deirdre Connelly, of Massachusetts, had a four-year-old son and was pregnant for the second time.

Transformational Breathing gave Deirdre the confidence to choose a birth technique some opposed. With trust in herself, the universe, and her midwife mother, she chose a water birth. She labored in the Jacuzzi tub for thirty-one minutes before delivering her six-pound, eight-ounce baby underwater. The birth video shows a calm, totally relaxed Deirdre breathing with each contraction and toning at the end as the baby slipped out and unfolded. We watched him lift his chin off his chest and rise to the surface where she held him in her arms and put him to the breast.

Deirdre later confirmed, "Transformational Breathing helped me to experience birth deeply, fully, and with utmost joy."

Infant Breath Session

At this time, too, there is a great opportunity to help the baby to integrate whatever trauma could not be avoided during the birth experience. Even if we have orchestrated a compassionate, sensitive birth experience, it will probably still be somewhat stressful. Birth and death are the two biggest transitions we ever go through.

Until the moment of birth, all our needs were automatically taken care of. Going from the security of the womb and the oneness with mother to being scared and in a plastic tub with a lot of other frightened and screaming newborn babies is rough! No wonder so many people have abandonment issues. It is a completely new experience to be cold, wet, hungry, and scared, and to have no way, other than crying, to communicate our needs.

Thus, one of the greatest gifts we can give a newborn is a breathing session shortly after emerging or perhaps after arriving at home. This gives babies the opportunity to clear negative emotions from the intensity of birth, so they don't have to carry them around for years thereafter.

I do not recommend doing this unless you have cleared your own birth trauma by having had at least a few Transformational Breathing sessions yourself. If possible, find a certified breath coach to facilitate the infant's first session. However, anyone who has enough experience with Transformational Breathing to feel comfortable doing so, would be fine. You cannot hurt a baby (or anyone) by breathing with them. Since the consciously-delivered newborn has a minimum of trauma to heal, the procedure is really quite simple and straightforward.

First of all, begin by communicating with the baby's soul and letting her know that she has the opportunity to clear birth trauma, and anything else that comes up. Let her know that you will help her if she so chooses. If the baby responds favorably (smiling, excited movement, eye contact, or an internal "yes"), find a comfortable place to sit, ideally a rocking chair, and sit the baby on your lap facing outward.

Put the fingers of both of your hands on each side of the baby's tummy and apply a little pressure. Then begin to breathe in an open, gentle, connected "circle." Soon the baby's breathing will begin to entrain to yours, easing into her stomach and abdominal areas. She may whimper and tense up a bit—both are signs of integrating birth trauma. Before too long, the baby will be breathing fully, in and out, in a relaxed, smooth rhythm.

Many colicky infants restrict their breathing to protect themselves from traumatic birth memory; they simply do not get enough Life Force into the belly area, thereby hindering digestion. This condition shifts dramatically after their breathing session. So remember this technique—it could help a little one you love a great deal!

"Breathing properly has opened my body and my awareness. Practicing daily took a little adjustment, as most things do. I no longer have an inhaler, I AM the inhaler. I live in Colorado, hiking comfortably at high altitudes daily. Breath is life, so live breathing! I am grateful."

Eligio Salvatore, age 19

14

Healing Respiratory Conditions

I find it very curious that modern medicine has not yet realized the value of working directly with the respiratory system in the treatment of respiratory symptoms. Sadly, when we seek medical help for a respiratory condition, we are usually just given inhalers and drugs indefinitely to treat the symptoms, often with no hope of actually addressing the cause to relieve the problem permanently. Considering the economy-driven society we live in, however, this is not really so surprising. Treatment modalities that cannot be patented by large pharmaceutical companies seldom reach mainstream awareness.

Many people who once suffered from asthma, emphysema, chronic bronchial infections, and even some rare lung and respiratory diseases have benefited greatly from Transformational Breathing. Over and over again, I have witnessed great improvements in their ability to breathe. Many eventually free themselves from a lifelong reliance on expensive, toxic, and sometimes debilitating drugs and oxygen-support systems.

The transformation process for chronic respiratory sufferers is a bit different than it is for the average person. For one thing, people with respiratory problems usually have a lifelong history of issues around breathing. In other words, not only is their breathing mechanism shut down, but they also tend to have many deep-seated negative beliefs and feelings that are *directly related* to the function of breathing itself. When this type of adverse relationship to one's most vital life-support system has been established, dysfunctional breathing patterns are deeply ingrained and do not shift easily.

The asthmatic breathing pattern is very easily recognized. Simply described, it is a continuous tightening of the muscles directly below the sternum (breastbone). This constriction prohibits the full release of the breath, especially in the upper chest.

Exhaling incompletely creates a situation in which the carbon dioxide (toxic waste) is not being expelled, so there is little or no room for the intake of new, cleansing, fresh oxygen. This cycle creates the feeling of not being able to get enough air. It has very little to do, however, with the popular medical belief that the lungs are unable to perform properly. It is simply a matter of not trusting enough to let go as we exhale and, thus, not having space for the next breath.

Naturally this pattern leads to a desperate need for fresh oxygen, particularly in the presence of any kind of physical or emotional stress, that requires extra oxygen for the body to function is present.

Over the years, I have personally assisted hundreds of individuals with respiratory challenges, primarily with the symptoms and diagnoses of asthma. One of my interests has been to note historical happenings that might be connected to their breathing disorders. During their breathing sessions, they often remember a trauma in infancy or childhood that originally caused the condition. Transformational Breathing allows these memories to surface and be integrated. Healing can then happen naturally.

A high percentage of my asthmatic clients suffered childhood trauma and pronounced feelings of mother-abandonment, sometimes dating all the way back to birth or earlier. A client may relive, for example, the panicked feeling caused by premature cutting of the umbilical cord, when oxygen supply was abruptly terminated, causing a life-threatening situation where the infant was forced to breathe or die.

Worse still, if the cord is wrapped around the infant's neck, an attitude of fear fills the room, and baby's breath patterns become firmly associated with this response. The most obvious abandonment scenario is being given up for adoption, an event that does not go unnoticed by the infant. In all of these situations, on some level, the confused infant desperately wonders, "Where's

Mommy? Why isn't she protecting and nourishing me? Why has she rejected me?"

Another recurring theme with asthmatic breathers is a fear or history of suffocation, drowning, or other life-threatening events in which a dramatic loss of air supply was experienced.

Such experiences set up what I call the asthmatic breathing pattern, putting into place the belief system that "I can never get enough." This subconscious belief not only greatly affects the breathing, but carries over into many other areas of life as well. Such people are usually engulfed by feelings that they cannot get enough love, attention, food, money, and energy.

During Transformational Breathing sessions, we have the advantage of re-experiencing those earlier moments of life now with a more mature level of understanding and a higher perspective of compassionate awareness. From this new multidimensional vantage point, painful judgments and assumptions can be reviewed and reframed into a loving perspective. The super-charged emotions associated with those beliefs are eliminated as well. Once this occurs, self-limiting associations are disengaged and transformed into forgiveness and even appreciation for Mother's as well as our own original perspective. Forgiveness releases the fear that causes the stress that triggers the respiratory attack.

Liz, for example, came to her first session believing she had an incurable condition. Her mother had left home when Liz was seven years old and her dad was busy healing his wounds and trying to fill the void. Liz adopted the belief that there was never enough for her. She learned to hold on to things–even to unpleasant thoughts and experiences—so that she might at least have plenty of *something*. She also held on to her breath, subconsciously believing that the next breath may not be coming. By the time she was thirty-three, Liz's breathing had become so restricted that she was diagnosed with asthma after being rushed to the emergency room.

Liz's asthma attack was the result of emotional and physical stress. The stress increased her body's demand for oxygen, and she panicked, believing she was unable to inhale enough air. The truth was that she was not able to *exhale* enough air—a necessity before new air can enter. This illustrated perfectly her unwillingness to let go of the negatives (toxins) in her life.

When the lungs are filled with toxins ready to be expelled, there is no room for nourishment (new oxygen) to enter, and the system auto-intoxicates—the toxins are recycled through the system. This leads to more stress—emotionally, physically, and ultimately to the reality of not having enough.

The fear of having asthma attacks now compounded the many scary beliefs that had been driving her behavior since birth. She experienced disease, pain, and many other harmful side effects. Her life was in a shambles. Yet as soon as Liz allowed for the possibility that she could transform her own breathing patterns and received proper guidance to do so, the whole direction of her life changed drastically.

During coached sessions, instead of continuing to struggle as she inhaled, she began to relax fully as she exhaled. This allowed room in the lungs for fresh air. With practice, her cycle of effort was eventually broken.

In Transformational Breathing sessions, Liz was able to clear the longstanding belief about life that there was never enough for her. She became aware of her habit of holding on to unpleasant thoughts and experiences. She realized and began to experience that letting go of what she did not need (but had been clinging to just to have something) made room for what she *really* wanted. She also found it easier to trust in her life as she discovered many new ways to let go of old fears.

Once she had cleaned out her closet, both literally and metaphorically, Liz found that more of what she really wanted could come in, and many struggles subsided. Behaviors and perspectives were effortlessly—sometimes automatically—modified. These new, more attractive and responsible behaviors and thoughts about life served to elicit more favorable responses from others. She soon found herself in an upward spiral of giving and receiving.

The irony is that this desperate holding on to the remnants of the last breath for fear of not getting another chance to inhale, creates exactly what is most feared. The next breath is thwarted because the first one has not been released! It becomes an insidious self-fulfilling prophecy, and a revealing example of our most common self-sabotage mechanism. We create that which we fear, and what we resist persists.

In Transformational Breathing sessions, we focus directly on training contracted muscles to relax as we exhale, so that the toxic carbon dioxide exits and there is space in the lungs for the next breath to enter. We also focus on reprogramming the mind to change the false negative beliefs about the ability to breathe, by affirming that it is safe to let go and that we each are worthy of plenty.

This process is self-regulated. The time it takes to change this or any other pattern depends in part upon how fervently we cling to our fear of freeing our breath.

In the first breathing session, asthmatic breathers are taught to recognize whether they are relaxing or holding on as they exhale. At the very least, this enables them to have the awareness of what intensifies the symptoms and allows them to begin to practice relaxing as they exhale. Usually by the fifth individual session, there is marked improvement in the ability to consciously release the breath during stressful times. As you can see, the progression with an asthmatic is somewhat slower than with someone who has no respiratory problems; yet compared to the allopathic alternative, Transformational Breathing provides new hope and renewed life.

Relaxing Asthmatic Symptoms

The following is a simple exercise that can be helpful in relaxing symptoms experienced by asthma sufferers. It is different from the Transformational Breathing and is not intended to replace it. It is especially important in cases of respiratory ailments to work with a certified Transformational Breathing facilitator for strong, clear coaching and support in the initial stages. This exercise can also be used on your own to gently begin to soften and relax the asthmatic breath pattern. It will assist in preparing you for the maximum benefit of your facilitated breathing sessions.

Begin by lying on your back, propped up at the shoulders to an angle between forty-five and seventy-five degrees. A wedge-shaped cushion or reclining chair is great for this as it supports you in relaxing and letting go.

Inhale a slow, deep breath through the nose. Place one or two fingers directly on the muscles just below the breastbone and apply enough pressure so the muscles relax. This area might be a bit tender at first due to accumulated tension, but it will feel better as it begins to relax. Exhale as quickly, freely, and gently as possible. A fully relaxed exhale is fast and easy; you may feel relieved, as if you are releasing a big weight. Consciously ask your body to relax, and keep feeling your diaphragm muscles. Feel the upper chest collapse as you release your breath. Don't be discouraged if this doesn't happen immediately. Remember, you are working with years of unproductive patterning. Repeat this for about ten minutes. Do this breath as quickly as you can while remaining soft and gentle in those muscles. Ideally, there are no pauses as you inhale and exhale.

When you can relax completely while breathing in and out with the nose, switch over to breathing in and out of the mouth in the same way.

Mandy's New Life

Several years ago, a client brought in his wife who had been suffering from severe asthma for the past twelve years. It was now at the stage where her difficulty in breathing was affecting and limiting most of her activities. She was only in her early thirties and was unable to work, exercise, or perform normal activities for someone her age. Her breathing was so restricted that she could not live an enjoyable life, and the asthma was the foremost consideration in everything they did.

Mandy was very pale and thin, always wheezing and quite listless. She was the most severe case I had ever worked with up to that point. Just lying down to breathe seemed to require all her energy. Her breathing pattern was very shut down. When I felt her solar plexus area, it was stiff as a board and felt hard all the time.

It didn't even relax as she inhaled, a sure sign she was holding on to something major.

I began patiently working on the muscles in that area, by gently applying pressure and massaging them with each breath. I was trying to teach them that it would be safe to relax and let go. At one point, I asked her to stop *trying* to breathe. I asked her instead to just let the breath come in and go out without any major effort. That was an important step toward beginning to breathe more effectively.

By the end of the first session, she could actually relax those controlling muscles during every fourth or fifth breath. Her face and cheeks had some color in them, and she said she felt totally energized. For the first time in quite a while, a greater amount of oxygen was entering her system and she was feeling the benefits.

I later learned that this coaching technique can assist many with asthma. I came to understand that the very act of trying so hard to breathe was causing much of the tension and constriction in the first place. Surrendering and relaxing, letting the breath flow in and flow out, allows our breathing to happen without the usual tightness and holding on.

We were both encouraged and we set her next appointment for two weeks later. I asked her to practice the relaxed, connected breathing for at least fifteen minutes a day.

In the second session, something very powerful occurred. Mandy's breath opened up enough for her to begin to activate, thus tapping in to the subconscious mind. After a short while, she began to cry hysterically. I asked her what was happening. In a few minutes, she regained her composure and was able to tell me that she had remembered a tragic event that had changed her life. She was surprised at how upset she still felt about it.

Twelve years previously, a young boy had run out in front of her car and, unable to stop, she had run him over. He was killed, and she was guilt-ridden. For a long time afterward, she thought she would never get over it. Unconsciously she felt that she did not deserve to live.

Immediately I connected that experience and her feelings about it with the onset of her asthma. Mandy had been denying herself life by subconsciously refusing to accept the Life Force through her own breathing. Before I could even voice my under-standing, I could see she had made the same association. We had accessed the emotional root of her debilitating breathing pattern.

The next few sessions continued to improve her breathing. On the fourth session, her husband came with her. They were both beaming as they shared with me that over the weekend they had gone bike riding together. She was actually able to go up hills and keep up with him, something they had never experienced in their relationship. They also stated that her need for the inhaler was almost nonexistent. When she felt difficulty breathing, she would instead stop and take ten deep, relaxed breaths. The exercises created enough opening in her breathing that the inhaler was not necessary. They were now planning events they had previously considered impossible, including plans to start a family.

Betty's Miraculous Healing

Several years ago, while working in New York with some young adults in the entertainment business, I witnessed one of the women break down and sob after her breath session. She told me that her mother was dying of a rare respiratory condition. Doctors had warned that there was no cure, and it would eventually kill her. She looked at me with a hopeful glance and asked if Transformational Breathing could help in any way. At that time I had no idea, and I explained to her that I had not heard of her mother's condition and did not know if it would respond to our work. I felt it was at least worth a try, and if they were willing to experiment, so was I.

Betty, in her mid-fifties, arrived in the city to meet with me the next day. In speaking with her, I gathered that she was not resigned to accepting the fatal prognosis, but she also felt lost as far as alternatives.

I explained the three levels of Transformational Breathing and let her know that we would probably be spending most of our time working on Level I, opening up her breathing. She seemed ready to try anything. I think that if I had recommended standing on her head and whistling she would have tried it.

When she started to breathe, I was amazed at how shut down her breathing was. There was no visible expansion of her chest as she inhaled. When I told her to take a deep breath, the air went in, but I saw almost no movement in her respiratory system. This type of breathing pattern is usually associated with feelings of unworthiness and the inability to accept one's good. I instructed her to continue to breathe and say, in her mind, "I accept my good. I am worthy of my good." As soon as I gave her that affirmation, she burst out in sobs. I knew I had struck a major chord.

After she stopped crying, there was visible expansion on her next breath. She was allowing herself to accept her good, her breath, her Life Force. As we continued the session, her breathing kept getting larger. I couldn't believe what I was seeing—that someone could go from a virtually non-existent breath to an open, healthy breathing pattern in less than an hour! I knew that by the end of our time together, her life was going to be very different.

When she sat up at the end of the session, she looked totally transformed. Her eyes were sparkling, her body was vibrating, and her smile told the whole story. We both knew some sort of miracle had happened, and I felt fortunate to be there and witness it.

Betty exclaimed, "I don't remember ever feeling quite so wonderful, so clear and light. It's as though I've never breathed before."

In talking to Betty later, I learned that she had been an unwanted child. Her mother had even considered aborting the pregnancy. She came into this world feeling unwanted and not worthy to be here—not even good enough to breathe. A lifetime of unconsciously believing herself to be unworthy of life and breath had caused a major shutdown of her respiratory system with detrimental consequences to her health. After one month of practicing the breathing exercises I had given her, Betty called to say she was doing fabulously well and did not feel a need for any more sessions. None of her medical practitioners could believe her miraculous recovery.

Not everyone's response is as dramatic as Betty's was. There are many factors that determine how quickly a person moves within this process. In part, it depends upon one's level of commit-

ment to practice, and readiness to heal, as well as the willingness to actively choose life.

Complete Recovery from Asthma

Shelley Salvatore has been a professional fitness instructor for sixteen years and was a dancer before that.

"As a teenager, I was diagnosed with asthma. Being strong-willed, I went through my life never needing medication, until my mid-thirties. My mother had died a few years earlier, and I was a single mother with fifteen- and sixteen-year-old sons who were going wild! I was teaching fifteen to twenty classes a week and diagnosed with exercise- induced asthma. The stress had finally caught up to my body.

"I was put on three types of medication that made me sick to my stomach and very hyper. I carried the inhalers with me, but knew that they were not the answer. Shortly thereafter (God bless!) I attended a Transformational Breathing workshop. After twenty minutes of deep, connected breathing, I knew that this was the answer to my prayers. I took the training, became a facilitator and my oldest son also did, with the scholarship program that Judith offers for teenagers. My younger son also breathes now. My breath is fuller than ever, my spiritual life has deepened and I am truly grateful for this gift—as simple as breathing consciously!"

Teenager Leaves Inhalers Behind

Eligio Salvatore, age nineteen, says: "My experience with Transformational Breathing was like sunshine on a cloudy day. At the age of ten, I was diagnosed with asthma after a serious bronchial infection. Two different types of inhalers were prescribed. One was steroid based and the other was Ventolin. I was told to use them daily (more than once) for the rest of my life.

"By nature, I am a rebel and decided at this young age that I could control my breath without depending on these drugs. I still had sporadic asthma attacks however. In the fall of 1996, I accompanied my brother and mother on a 'breath retreat,' where I was reintroduced to spirit, mind, body, and, most importantly, my breath. Breathing properly has opened my body and my awareness. Practicing daily took a little adjustment, as most things do. I now strive to be aware of my breath on a constant basis. I've learned to breathe into the NOW. Also, I no longer have an inhaler, I AM the inhaler. I live in Colorado (the mile-high state), hiking comfortably at high altitudes daily. Breath is life, so live breathing! I am grateful."

Transformational Breathing has a great deal to contribute to the field of respiratory health. Current medical treatments tend to be effect-oriented and quite toxic. Drugs merely control symptoms and offer little in the way of permanent change or healing. Transformational Breathing offers a whole new self-responsible approach to the treatment of respiratory conditions.

Addressing breathing patterns, and changing them, gives one the ability to be proactive and to participate in the healing process. It offers the potential for physical as well as emotional healing of underlying causes, by accessing and integrating repressed beliefs and trauma. This leads to true rehabilitation.

*"I feel truly connected and happy.
It has been fifteen months since I have smoked
a cigarette, and I've lost my taste for alcohol.
I feel confident to step forward..."*

Aja Salvatore, Age 18

15

The Natural High

Over the past twenty years, I have witnessed and worked with many people struggling with some type of substance addiction. Some came to me specifically to work on drug abuse issues, and others came for different reasons. Not everyone was entirely successful; however, a good percentage were astonished at their rapid and lasting success.

A good example is Lorna Tobin, who left home at fourteen years of age and lived with a foster family for two years before moving out on her own. She had been sexually, physically, and emotionally abused, and was addicted to amphetamines, cocaine, and cigarettes. Soon after getting married and having a child, she started seeing a psychologist for severe depression. He prescribed anti-depressants which parlayed into anti-anxiety medication and sleeping pills. She ended up addicted to them as well. Her psychiatrist sexually abused her in therapy, which contributed to her divorce.

Lorna began doing private breathing sessions with Charyl Ozkaya in 1994, and they continued for six months on a weekly basis:

I was amazed at the transformation of my life. I soon started to feel relaxed and to feel love for myself. I quit smoking. I stopped taking the drugs too. I began allowing myself to cry when I needed to—something I could never do before. I once had cysts in my thyroid that had to be aspirated every few months. They are no longer there.

I am a different person since I started. I have let go of all the layers of pain and my life is now full of love, peace and joy. This gives me the ability to really be there for my son, on all levels, as I have resolved my own childhood trauma and am now able to see him for who he is—no longer as a reflection of my own pain.

I don't know where I would be today if I had not chosen this path—probably dead, as I had attempted suicide many times. Thinking about that part of my life now, it is difficult to even imagine being the same person. Transformational Breathwork saved me. I truly feel that the breath is the most powerful healing tool available today.

In his highly informative book, *Oxygen Therapies; A New Way of Approaching Disease* (Energy Publications, 1998), Edward McCabe explains how "alcohol and drug cravings are reduced significantly by oxygenation." He provides the following sensible hypothesis which may go a long way toward explaining the success in overcoming addictions often experienced by Transformational Breathers.

Any body craving is a signal that there is a condition of 'too much of something' in the cells. The craving is for the intake of that something's opposite for balance. We now hear from scientists that most alcoholics are genetically predisposed to having certain compounds in their bodies that make them crave alcohol. These compounds build up, ready to dissolve alcohol, and if there is no alcohol, they [demand] you get some. If the cells storing these sub-stances at the ready are cleaned up by oxygenation and returned to the childhood DNA state of cleanliness—if there is no more of that substance in the body creating an imbalance—where will the craving come from?

I do not yet understand why breathing is an effective tool for full recovery for some and not for others. It could reflect the individual's level of commitment. It may simply be a matter of timing and one's readiness for change. Or perhaps the answer lies in the complexity of the problem itself. Overall, the results I have seen in healing addictions have been very encouraging.

The biggest challenge in working with addictive personalities is getting their bodies to a session. Transformational Breathing has brought remarkable results to those who truly desired freedom from addictions. Hundreds have reclaimed fulfilling lives after years of bondage to cigarette smoking, severe alcohol and drug abuse, long-term daily marijuana use, and other addictive patterns such as overeating, gambling, and sex addiction. Once they arrive and begin to breathe, the healing is generally quite rapid.

My experience has shown me that most drug abusers are attempting to find their innate higher intelligence. Marijuana and certain other chemical drugs are known to bring the feeling of deeper awareness or profound meaning into even the most mundane of topics and activities. For many years, the psychoactive properties of LSD were studied by psychiatric research scientists. In fact, this was where Dr. Stanislav Grof found his entry into the holotropic world of cosmic consciousness.

In his book, *The Holotropic Mind*, Grof recalls his own experience as a test subject in 1956:

> *I agreed to have my brain waves monitored by electroencephalograph [EEG] while lights of various frequencies were flashed before my eyes. I was hit by a radiance that seemed comparable to the light at the epicenter of an atomic explosion, or possibly to the supernatural light described in Oriental scriptures that appears at the moment of death. This thunderbolt of light catapulted me from my body. There was no doubt in my mind that what I was experiencing was very close to experiences of cosmic consciousness I had read about in the great mystical scriptures of the world. [It was] a glimpse beyond ordinary reality.*

Happily, LSD is not needed to gain such glimpses. Nor is marijuana or any other substance. Although a breathing session is much gentler and more easily controlled by the breather than any drug-induced trip, it can and does lead to similar profound states of awareness. And there is no crash or hangover with breathing, as there is with the roller coaster stress that unnatural drugs place on the system. To the contrary, the only physical side effects of breathing are happy blood cells and abundant energy.

Drug abuse can also result from trying to cover up or push away disturbing feelings that are attempting to surface. Alcohol in particular is known either to relax the drinker enough to let go and have a good time or to bring out another side of the personality altogether. Many so-called obnoxious drunks who get loud, confrontational, and emotional are often subdued, depressed, and/ or self-conscious when sober. They tend to repress feelings on a stringently regular basis. Alcohol then relaxes their inhibitions, allowing pent-up feelings to be expressed.

Of course, there are much safer places and more effective ways to express pent-up feelings. The safest place is in a breath session with a qualified, non-judgmental coach. Once emotional and biochemical balance is restored, it is no longer necessary to attempt to compensate with artificial means such as drugs.

I recently received this letter from a female graduate of our Personal and Professional Training Program, conveying how Transformational Breathing assisted her recovery from a long battle with alcoholism.

> *Dear Judith,*
>
> *I am writing this letter to let you know how much the Transformational Breathing has helped me with a certain problem. I have struggled with alcohol for most of my life— at least thirty years. I had certain periods in my life when I was sober, but eventually I always slipped back into drinking. First it would be for special occasions, then socially, and pretty soon it was out of control again.*
>
> *I originally took the breath training to help with my asthma and the difficulty I have had breathing. My breathing has improved greatly. But also throughout the course of the training program, I received some changes I did not expect. I lost the desire to drink. It wasn't even anything I thought about. I just did not want to drink anymore. It has been two years since I have had anything to drink—or even wanted to. This is a great blessing to me and to my*

family. Words can't express how grateful we are and how different my life is now.

Thank you for the work you do and for helping so many. I hope this letter will inspire others to be willing to try the breath program and gain so much as well.

Sincerely,

Barbara Jo McCormick

Oxygen is essential for the biological release and distribution, via the bloodstream, of such secretions as endorphins, enkephalins, serotonin, neuropeptides, and hormones. These organic chemicals produce blissful and euphoric states. Some of them are responsible for the high that dancers and athletes regularly experience; many rely upon it for that proverbial second wind after coming to the point of exhaustion in a race or contest. Other chemicals are released in abundance during exquisite experiences such as massage, a sunset, a tender embrace, or a sensual encounter. These natural secretions are certainly more powerful and healthier than any manmade chemical or organic substance commonly ingested to get high.

On many occasions, clients and workshop participants finish their breath sessions exclaiming, "Wow, this is better than any drug I ever took!" The real beauty of a *breather's high* is that, unlike a drug high, it is healthy, self-generated, and often permanent. No dealer or pharmaceutical company is needed. And no great exertion is required as it is to achieve a "runner's high".

Chances are that if you've been drinking and drugging, your body can't possibly endure the rigors of strenuous exercise anyway, even if you could summon up the self-discipline to throw on a pair of sneakers and do it! Fortunately, Transformational Breathing is a lying-down sport that we can all manage—even the elderly or very sick.

The ecstatic highs of super-oxygenating one's system can become addictive, but there are no negative side-effects or consequences as in substance addiction. Breathing is nontoxic, regenerating, inexpensive, expansive, and self-regulating. It's also free once you learn to facilitate your own sessions! Don't be surprised if you soon acquire the self-love and self-discipline to establish a regular exercise regimen in addition to all the other healthy benefits.

Addictive behaviors must be addressed and resolved at the level of cause. Many of us have never fully outgrown the period of unfulfilled needs of the small child self. Some important aspects of self-esteem and self-caring (which ideally develop as we mature into adults) have stayed behind, locked in the infancy stage. As a result, development is arrested and energy is trapped in those areas of repression where our needs were not met. Recognizing those unfulfilled needs empowers us to see and heal them from the perspective of a capable adult.

Shirley, a woman in her late thirties, came to me specifically to stop smoking. She had been struggling for many years with a compulsive desire to smoke. Her three young children were getting to the age where they were beginning to mimic their mom. She was afraid that soon they would want to smoke as well. She ate well, exercised, and yet this smoking habit lingered, totally incongruent with the rest of her life. She had tried everything that was available, from hypnosis to nicotine patches, and nothing ever worked for more than a few days.

When she came for her appointment, I could see both the hope and the exasperation in her eyes. Not long into her first breathing session, she started making a sucking motion with her mouth. It got stronger and stronger, until it seemed to fill the whole room. Shirley was visibly making large sucking motions with her mouth.

What happened next surprised me even more. I began to feel a strong urge to suck as well, and I actually found myself making sucking motions inside my own mouth. I wondered what she was integrating. At one point she started to cry, and I saw this as an opportunity to ask her what was happening. She opened her eyes and told me she was sad because she was experiencing herself as a baby who needed to nurse. She said her mom was unwilling and she had this unfulfilled sucking urge that was stronger than anything she had ever felt. Based on the sucking energy that had filled the room, I believed her!

As she continued to breathe, she began to understand the reasons her mom would not nurse, and soon a loving compassion for her mother replaced the unfulfilled need. Before long, the sucking urges dissipated and she continued to breathe in a new way. Somehow her breath had opened up fully and seemed effortless. She coughed up a lot of mucus during the course of the session, and I watched her lungs exercise vigorously for about forty-five minutes. It appeared to be a diligent effort to correct any damage from the cigarette smoking.

At the end of the session, she sat up and declared how great she felt. She understood why she had not been able to quit smoking on her own. Several weeks later, I ran into her at a basketball game and asked how things were going. She beamed with pride that she hadn't had one cigarette or even the desire to smoke since the day of her session. I saw her again three years later and she was still a nonsmoker.

It's interesting to note that smoking a cigarette provides a temporary lift, partly because it takes the focus off rising emotions—particularly fear and anger—and stuffs them back down. Tar temporarily anesthetizes the alveoli, and nicotine gives a unique sort of high. However, if you take notice, you'll find that inhaling the smoke is often accompanied by a deep breath—perhaps the deepest, most deliberate breath a smoker ever takes is when he is smoking. Could it be that the deep breath is actually responsible for that coveted release of tension?

By integrating, clearing out, and healing undeveloped or false aspects of the self, Transformational Breathing gives us experiential evidence that we have unlimited internal access to the emotional and spiritual highs sometimes sought in mind-altering substances. It reconnects us with the Source of our own spiritual nature without drugs and without unhealthy side effects. Spiritual bankruptcy is history once we've seen the Higher Perspective firsthand—that true fulfillment comes from giving and receiving love, from developing inner strength and from appreciating and sharing our unique talents and qualities.

I remember one client with a long history of cocaine addiction who had been in recovery for several years. After his first breathing session he told me with tears in his eyes that he had just had his first real experience of Higher Power. After years of referring to his

Higher Power on a daily basis at Twelve-Step meetings and while working his program for recovery, he finally knew what It was. Higher Power was no longer just a vague concept to him, but a powerful reality. This awesome experience is actually quite typical.

The more we experience our own clear connection with Higher Power, God, Holy Spirit, Universal Consciousness, Creator—or whatever name you prefer in referring to the Divine—the more faith we develop in ourselves and in life itself. True faith leads to true peace and joy because faith is the realization that it's all good—all of life is a gift and a blessing. The effects of drugs cannot even compare with such knowing. As we allow fulfillment to bubble up from within, the desire for external stimulation naturally subsides.

16

Breathing with Youngsters

I have had some amazing experiences facilitating Transforma-tional Breathing sessions with children. In many ways, breathing with children is very similar to breathing with adults. There are some distinct differences as well. Repressions integrate very quickly for children, primarily because they have had less time to build layer upon layer of repressed material. Perhaps due to this comparatively minimal buildup, which blocks the view to our inner landscape, children seem to be more readily in touch with their subconscious minds and inner worlds.

One of the most important factors in conducting successful breath sessions with children is motivation. Unless some type of leverage is established initially, it can be difficult to keep them focused on the breath. Sometimes children are self-motivated by the desire to be free of negative emotional experiences, such as nightmares, anger toward siblings, and overwhelming fears. Others can be inspired by some of the apparent physical benefits of better breathing, such as improved performance in sports, having more energy, better health and happier relationships. In some circum-stances, offering a reward for breathing is effective.

Parents play an important role in their children's sessions. Sometimes it is crucial to have a parent present, and other times it is better not to have them there. I have found that the young person is usually quite clear about the appropriateness of having their parent there or not, so I ask the young person what their preference is. Most choose to have the parent there, but the parent must be willing to honor the child's choice in either case.

One of the greatest joys in working with children is knowing that if they learn to breathe openly and effectively while they are young, many of the problems caused by dysfunctional breathing will be avoided throughout their lives. As conscious breathers trained early, they can escape many of the common ailments resulting from poor breathing and enjoy a healthier life. Another wonderful advantage is that, as emotional patterns are integrated, the very basis for the toxic snowballing of negativity, as discussed earlier, is eliminated. Having acquired the invaluable tool of conscious breathing, they are equipped and free to continue clearing out negativity for the rest of their lives. Clearing the subconscious at an early age immensely improves quality of life.

As a mother of ten (birth mother of eight and stepmother of two), grandmother of five, and a person who has specialized in working with children over the past twenty-five years, I have seen some amazing things happen in breathing sessions with my young clients. Here are some of the most memorable experiences.

Battling Memories of War

Nine-year-old Katie had been adopted as a toddler from Korea. The only child in her adoptive family, she was extremely wanted and loved. Her mother had been in one of my earlier training programs and a student in many of my metaphysical classes. One day she came to me and shared deep concerns about Katie, who was having terrifying nightmares regularly. Katie's birth parents had died during the Korean War, and Katie had no conscious memory of them or of Korea. It was apparent that she had been heavily traumatized during those first few years of her life in a war zone. Her mother was at a loss. Could Transformational Breathing give her some assistance in integrating whatever trauma was there?

During Katie's interview. I asked her if she wanted her mother to be present during the session and she did. Her breathing analysis revealed that Katie was a deep breather, but she did not breathe into her belly at all. I pressed my hand lightly on her belly and gently encouraged her to breathe there.

As the breathing moved into the lower respiratory system, she began to get very scared and began sobbing hysterically. Some of the memories of war experiences were surfacing, and she finally felt safe enough to feel them fully. We all knew that within this expression lay her freedom. For the next forty minutes, she went through a lot of terror and sadness. Her mother did not seem surprised at the depth of her daughter's pain. At the end of the session, it was a relief to see the peace and joy so vibrant in Katie's eyes. We agreed that Katie would continue breathing with her mother. Several weeks later, I received a call. Katie had had no nightmares since her first session, and she was much happier at home and at school. She also said she looks forward to her breathing homework and sessions.

Attention Deficit Disorder

Another of my adult clients was concerned about her daughter, who had had a difficult birth. Little ten-year-old Simone was bright, cheery, and restless. She had been diagnosed with Attention Deficit Disorder and was experiencing difficulty in school. She wanted to do better at school—a valid intention for her breathing session.

Unlike Katie, Simone breathed well into her belly, but there was no movement in her upper chest. We had her do a two-stroke inhalation, which immediately brought her breath into the upper chest. Soon the two strokes merged into a single full breath.

Simone wiggled and moved her body quite a bit while breathing. She also commented on feeling lots of tingling in her head and chest throughout the session, which otherwise seemed somewhat uneventful. Her breathing continued in an intense fashion, but compared to Katie, she was apparently devoid of emotion. At the end, Simone was lying in a very peaceful state, breathing in a slow connected pattern.

There is a point toward the end of every Transformational Breathing session when the client is peaceful and open. At this time, we ask the person's Higher Self to give the client a clear sign of connection. When I work with younger people, I ask that their angel self connect with them. This is what I did with Simone. What happened next was unbelievable, and I can only be thankful that her mother was there to witness it, for on the center of her forehead there appeared a reddish-orange splotch in the exact shape of an angel.

Simone's mother later told me that the angel symbol stayed on her forehead for three days after the session. She also was happy to report that Simone had been doing her breathing homework and was finding it much easier to focus in school and at home. Her mother also said she found Simone to be more loving. They both felt that the Transformational Breathing was reducing the ADD symptoms immensely.

Solomon Remembers

My son Solomon had a very homey birth in our rambling old cape house in Maine. It was the middle of July and seven of his siblings (five of my own children and my partner's two sons) were standing around, sitting on the bed, and wandering in and out experiencing various stages of shock and joy.

It was such a natural and joyous occasion. It felt so right to have the whole family there to welcome this handsome, bright-eyed new baby. He felt all the love and support and did not fuss or seem upset. He was just happy to finally be with all of us.

On Mother's Day, when Solomon was eight , he climbed up on my bed where I was relaxing and waiting for my traditional breakfast in bed. In a matter-of-fact tone he said, "Mom, I want to do a breathing with you."

Never passing up an opportunity to breathe with one of the children, I put my hand on his belly and we began. After about ten minutes, he made a contorted face and said his tummy hurt. I reassured him and told him to keep breathing. A few minutes later, the biggest grin appeared on his face. Smiling ear to ear, he looked up at me and said, "My belly feels so tingly and good. I see all my brothers and sisters there to welcome me. I'm so happy to be here."

He then popped up out of bed and went into the kitchen for pancakes. A short while later, he came back in and asked me if he could breathe again. A satisfied customer indeed!

Little Teddy "Bweathes"

At two, Teddy was the youngest member of a professional family with whom I was working. His mother and father are chiropractors, his grandfather is a psychologist, and his grandmother is a school administrator. I visited them regularly, working not only with the adults, but with their five-year-old daughter as well, who had suffered with terrible bouts of anger and jealousy since Teddy was born.

Each time I visited, Teddy would come up to me and ask, "I bweathe now?" I would joke back, "Next time, Teddy." Then one day I realized that something in him sincerely wanted to breathe. So at the end of that day, I told him it was his turn.

His sweet little face beamed with pride as he marched into the breathing room with me. Lying down next to me, he grabbed the end of my necklace and started playing with it. I demonstrated the circular breathing pattern to him which he continued easily for almost 45 minutes. I was amazed at his ability to focus and stay with the breathing. Then almost as quickly as he began, he stopped, and I knew we were done. He had not gone through any emotional releases, but I could see certain places of tension and stress resolving during the session.

When we walked out of the room, his parents and older sister were waiting for us. He had that unmistakable look of accomplishment in his eyes. As we all headed for the other room, the two children were in front of us. Big sister put her arm around Teddy's shoulders, looked him squarely in the eyes and asked, "So how was your bweathing session?" It was one of the cutest things I had ever seen—definitely a sign of the times. I felt honored to be a part of three generations healing the gap together.

Young Man Bound for Jail

Danny's stepmother was enrolled in our Maryland training program. His dad, whom I had not met, called me at home one evening. Sounding quite desperate, he said that Danny (not his real name), who lived in the Boston area with his mom, was in big trouble and had a long history of mental and emotional disturbances. He wanted to see if the breathing might help. He and his wife had tried everything they could think of and nothing seemed to help. Danny had been prescribed numerous medications for suspected schizophrenia. They were also afraid that at the age of 16 he might be tried and sentenced as an adult for a teenage fight in which one of the other kids had been badly hurt.

I agreed to see Danny upon the condition that he was willing to do the breathing. When they arrived at my office in Boston, he was visibly stressed,—to say the least. He paced my office floor like a caged animal. It was impossible for him to make eye contact or even sit down. When I asked him questions, his answers were short and unfocused. His eyes darted everywhere but never met mine.

This young man was obviously deeply troubled. I knew that the sooner we could begin the breathing, the better, for Danny was unreachable in his current state.

He went deep into the process very quickly, and I could see he was processing some very intense feelings by the look of agony on his face. His session lasted almost two hours—as if some part of him wanted to take full advantage of the opportunity to heal and clear as much as possible.

Of all the sessions I've ever facilitated, I have never experienced such profound transformation as in that first session with Danny. When he was done, he sat up with tears in his eyes. Making full eye contact with me and smiling, he shared many of the realizations he had gained during his session. He said he had found great understanding and forgiveness during those two hours, and he knew that he was now very different. There was a sense of peace that filled him.

Danny and I did a few more sessions, and the reports from his father filled me with awe for this process. His whole way of being had become more peaceful and inwardly reflective. At the end of the third session I recommended to his father that Danny take the training program, especially since he wasn't able to attend school at that time.

Danny became one of the first teenagers to enroll in and graduate from the TBF personal and professional training program. He soon started doing Transformational Breathing sessions with his friends and realized that he had something very wonderful to give and share.

During the course of the training program, Danny went to court on the pending legal matter. It was determined that he would be tried as a juvenile, and because his demeanor and behavior had changed so much, he was given a suspended sentence and probation. This was a dramatic demonstration of how intentional breathing can turn a young life totally around, going from destructive anti-social behavior to being a positive force in the world.

Sexual Abuse Uncovered

One of my friends was helping to raise her five-year-old granddaughter who had been having a lot of difficulty. Sherry was acting out sexually, wetting the bed, and continuously sucking her thumb. She was particularly upset and engaged in these troubling behaviors whenever she returned from visits with her mother. And when it was time to return to visit her mother, Sherry always resisted. My friend suspected some type of sexual abuse, but Sherry would only cry when questioned. My friend was petitioning the court for custody of Sherry, due to her daughter's drug involvement and the parade of men floating in and out of her life.

My friend asked me to try Transformational Breathing with Sherry to see if it would help and perhaps shed some light on what was happening. She also asked me to tape the breath session in case Sherry said anything revealing.

Sherry followed my instructions very well—we had built a substantial relationship of love and trust over the years. Shortly into the session, she began to shiver and act quite afraid. We asked her what was happening. She kept crying, "Leave me alone!" and saying "No!" over and over again. After a fair amount of time encouraging her to share her experience with us, she began to describe scenes of sexual abuse. Much to our shock and horror, it was the mother who had been abusing Sherry.

Even though the tape was not admissible in court, my friend did play it for Sherry's guardian, who then made a recommendation to the court for the grandmother to retain legal custody with only supervised visitation for the mother. Sherry's behaviors and happiness improved with the combined effects of conscious breathing and the positive changes in her life.

Teenage Facilitators

Following the successful completion of the training program by Danny and my daughter Madonna (both at age 16), I realized that there was a definite place for young people in this program. At that point, I was guided to make scholarships available for teenagers who wanted to attend the training program. To date, we have had at least one or two teenagers in almost every program.

Watching the changes and empowerment of these young people during that four-weekend journey has been one of the greatest gifts I have received from this work. I am still amazed at their ability to be present and participate at the same level as the adults. It seems as though the great spirits in these young bodies are coming to remember who they are. It is awe-inspiring to hear at each session how their lives have changed during the previous month. I am incredibly encouraged to see how quickly they open up and claim their place and power as healers.

The following are just a few of many letters from teenage graduates who share how Transformational Breathing has affected their lives.

Aja Salvatore was seventeen when his mother, a friend and certified facilitator from Connecticut, was concerned about his history with drugs and trouble with the authorities. Here is his story in his own words:

Somewhere around the age of twelve or thirteen, I
entered what felt like a period of total blackness. I felt like
my teachers were lying to me, and many of my classmates

were already gearing up for a lifetime of materialism intertwined with corporate America.

Being raised by a single mom, I felt a lot of pain and frustration about the absence of a real male role model. I was searching for what I thought it meant to be a man. I found myself emulating older men and boys, many of them black, who were probably more pissed off than I was. We were bound by what we thought was poverty, and the lust for the materialism that was all around us in wealthy Greenwich, Connecticut.

In my reality, these were men—real men—tough as nails, saying whatever they wanted to say. Physical force was the obvious and immediate answer. At the age of fourteen, I spent ten months in a boys' home with boys older and younger than me. Most of them came from horrible neighborhoods in cities such as Bridgeport, New Haven, and Hartford. Doing this time served no other purpose than to quadruple my anger and frustration. It also gave me twice as much criminal knowledge.

I drank heavily to kill my pain. I also began to experiment with psychedelic drugs. From that experimenting, a seed was planted. On acid, the world appeared as I thought it should—it was extremely beautiful. The major drawback was that the feeling only lasted six hours. I spent the next two years working and drinking heavily to cope with life and the law, which had once again caught up with me for drugs.

Soon I was under the thumb of a pretty uptight female probation officer who seemed to dictate the circumstances of my life. For someone like me, who had always seemed to have a real authority problem, that situation almost broke me. I knew I wanted an alternative lifestyle with real spiritual meaning. About this time, my mom mentioned the possibility of a scholarship for the breathwork she had been doing. She urged me to try a session first.

Ten minutes into the breathing revealed that I was breathing backwards and sent me into an intense case of tetany. It also showed me that Transformational Breathing was something I wanted to know more about. That was when I met Judith, and those were the circumstances of my life that led me to the training, which is still, to date, the most intense four months of my life.

Needless to say, there was an intense power at work and I could not deny it. I listened carefully, and was especially fond of Judith's open-mindedness to exploration. I learned to use the tools she gave me to explore my own consciousness. By the end of the training, I was seeing life in a whole new reality.

Things were definitely looking up as well. My probation officer agreed to let me move and even made a motion to dismiss my case. I made plans to leave home and do some of the traveling I had wanted so badly to do. The thought of leaving the love and security of the weekend intensives each month for the previous four months, however, left me feeling like a newborn baby in a hospital—wrenched from the womb. I could never go backwards [to my old way of life] and live with myself, and the thought of being the only one responsible for my happiness seemed overwhelming.

Doing the breathing again during this past six months has reshaped my reality. I have finally begun to see the world in a manner of perfection. I need only to breathe and be happy and strive for happiness, and things will change for the better. I can be the example, not the preacher—then people can't help but be swept up in that energy. I feel truly connected and happy. It has been fifteen months since I have smoked a cigarette and I've lost my taste for alcohol. I feel confident to step forward and be, in many ways, a leader—as we are all capable [of being]. I am and I love.

I still facilitate sessions from time to time. Those people give me very positive feedback on my ability to help others heal themselves.

I have to say thank you, Judith, from the bottom of my heart. Breathing continues to change my life and always will. The world is changing and I feel it!

Cindy Merrit was eighteen when she experienced her first Transformational Breathing sessions, facilitated by Aja. She wrote me a letter expressing how much she wanted to join the training program. We accepted her request, and she entered the Long Island training. One year later, she wrote this:

Since I was first introduced to Transformational Breathing, there have been major shifts in my life. The first was forgiving myself for holding on to my father even though he has never been around for me. Once I released him, I began to realize how much I have to be thankful for. When this lesson of forgiving and letting go took place, enormous amounts of love and compassion began to flow endlessly through me.

I have never before felt so uplifted and connected to my Self. Because of this connection, my consciousness has been raised and I now live in the present moment instead of dwelling in the past. No longer do I worry or stress about outcomes, because everything always seems to work out. All I have to do is trust. Now that my breath is fully open, likewise my mind, I am in the flow of life.

At the tender age of fourteen, Carolyne LaCerte entered the training program with her mother. Eva had raised Carolyne as a single parent since birth. The closeness and bonding that grew between them throughout the training was awe-inspiring. Many times in their sharing, one could observe the switching of parent-child roles and the deepening of their relationship as a result.

Carolyne's age did not affect her ability to participate or facilitate in any part of the training. In fact, she was the first of fifteen in that graduating class to achieve certification. She has since given sessions and workshops for her friends at school, and she is the first to admit that this has dramatically changed her life. This is what she shared about her breathing journey:

Transformational Breathing is a miracle to yourself that sits right in front of you. The breath has brought me to a higher consciousness which has helped me through depression, attempted suicide, and daily living as an adolescent. It has brought me the light of God into myself and helped me to look at all aspects of life—especially myself—from a different perspective.

The breath has brought more Prana [Life Force energy] into my body which allows me to release the suppressed feelings inside and become more connected with the soul. The breath has brought all joyful belongings to me. I feel I am becoming more ... whole.

I realize that my physical appearance tells me about what's going on inside myself. It has been a wonder to share the breathing with many people. I am here to give, and Transformational Breathing is a way I have chosen that fits with my personality. It is a wordless, never-ending offering of joy that is one of the best things that ever happened to me. I thank all my teachers who led me on [this] healthy starting process.

Up until a certain age (usually twelve), children often take on their parents' breathing patterns. These patterns reflect their parents' issues, which children carry around in addition to their own. Therefore, it is a good idea for the parents of children who get into breathing to practice it as well. As parents clear their issues, their children, too, will benefit.

A perfect example of this was a mother who had brought her son to me to help resolve his anger. He was constantly in trouble at school, losing his temper, and throwing angry fits at home. We did several breath sessions.

I coached him to pound and kick on pillows to get his breathing activated and to provide a safe means to express some of his pent-up anger. Eventually he shared that he was very angry at his father who had left the family a few years earlier and spent little time with him since.

Knowing that children do absorb and act out parental issues, I approached his mother and encouraged her to do some breathing as well. She was willing to do whatever she could to help her son and wisely did not rule out having some responsibility for her son's emotional state.

During her first session, I noticed that she and her son had almost identical breathing patterns, with hers a bit more pronounced and fixed than his. They both held on to the breath in the upper chest, the primary place where anger is stored. They both tended to rock their pelvic area during exhalation, a form of body language that showed they were holding on to past trauma.

Mom confided to me that she was surprised at how much anger she had felt toward her ex-husband during the session, having thought she had healed it long ago. By the end of the session, she said she felt much better—emotionally "freed up."

During my next session with her son, his upper chest was no longer holding on, and he did not feel the anger anymore. Somehow his mother's healing of her angry feelings had transferred to him and he had received a healing as well.

When my children were younger, taking a time out when they were having a hard time with themselves or their siblings meant going to a quiet spot and breathing. It was amazing how quickly their attitudes would shift after doing what we call *100 Breaths to Joy.* Sometimes they would try to fake it and pretend they had done the breathing; however, we could always tell, by their tone of voice, if they had done the breathing or not. At first, they would resent having to breathe as a consequence. But soon it became a welcome reprieve from some unconscious negative behavior.

In our family meetings, we would remind the children to take several deep breaths and count to ten before responding in anger. We encouraged them to feel their feelings during the breathing, without feeling the need to act them out. I have since found out that many children's programs in schools, group homes, and treatment centers use the same means for anger management and healthy expression of anger.

A number of graduates from the program are teachers in public and private schools and have shared aspects of conscious breathing in their work. Feeling they were on shaky new territory, they each proceeded slowly and cautiously in the school settings. They all reported positive results with the children in the form of being more peaceful, centered, and focused. The key was to present it in a non-threatening way, so as not to upset years of bureaucratic educational tradition.

Some of the teachers got discouraged and discontinued. Others patiently moved through the restrictive atmosphere of the public educational system environment.

The Golden Years:
Aging and Longevity

After his fourth Transformational Breathing session—my gift to him on his ninety-first birthday—the late Dr. Benjamin Spock told me, "I feel so good, much more relaxed and more alive at the same time." The twinkle in his eye was beaming bright and he seemed more vibrant than ever. Sessions with Dr. Spock were pretty effortless yet very powerful, as he always ventured willingly and deeply into the process.

We had met at Deepak Chopra's center in San Diego where Ben's devoted wife Mary had heard others exclaiming about their breath sessions. She was very astute and wanted Ben to try it so that he could remain as healthy and energetic as possible during his remaining years. He enjoyed it so much that they invited me to their home in Maine, where they both enjoyed several more sessions. I believe I enjoyed the sessions just as much as they did and feel quite blessed to have shared such sacred times with such wise and gentle souls.

It has always been an exceptional pleasure for me to breathe with seniors, who enjoy a vast array of benefits from breathwork, including reduced pain, renewed health, and major shifts in energy levels and attitudes. It is truly inspirational to observe this healing. Because of the decline in these attributes as we get older, the positive changes appear more extreme and dramatic with seniors.

In her book *The Nutrition and Dietary Consultant*, Sonya C. Starr, B.S., N.C., states: "When there is a lack of oxygen, the body is unable to assimilate vitamin C properly. There is a collagen breakdown. A lack of oxygen is why body organs grow old, permitting arteries and veins to harden. It is also the primary cause of strokes and degeneration of the brain."

Many seniors rely solely on the advice of medical doctors, who are trained to rely primarily on drugs. The medical and pharmaceutical fields have only recently begun exploring profitable ways to prescribe oxygen as treatment for disease.

The Hyperbaric Oxygen Chamber is a new and expensive technology being tested and used sparsely in the United States. Like all unnatural approaches to treatment, there are side effects and issues of safety and efficiency to contend with, but the news is encouraging.

Far less expensive and safer is the science of conscious breathing. Even so, some seniors believe that it's too late for them to change or perhaps too much for them to go digging around in the past. Certainly years of experience can be a two-sided coin. The buildup of repressed emotions and self-fulfilling belief systems piled on year after year can give the illusion of being an impossible mountain to climb. Yet there is a certain level of self-acceptance that also comes with maturity and *this* is the key to rapid change.

A good breath session can transform any depth of pain, anguish, and ingrained patterns. The key to rapid success, however, is the willingness to let go and allow the process to take place without resistance—without judging ourselves or whatever takes place. This is where the senior citizen has the advantage as compared to a younger person.

Teenagers, for example, may not have as much buildup but may be in that self-conscious stage which hinges on peer pressure and makes it hard for them to let go as easily. They might be more concerned about keeping their hair from getting messy than finding inner peace. Not so with the mature adult. The focus has long since shifted from "How do I appear?" to "How do I feel?" And this is the perspective from which one is most open to rapid results with Transformational Breathing. Forget about how you look, focus on how you feel, breathe deeply and fully, and soon you will look and feel much younger and happier.

ReHanna Rich is a woman in her late seventies who no longer looks or acts her age. "I am learning that the way I breathe is a barometer of how I live my life," she says, after using Transformational Breathing for several years and sharing it as a facilitator with many others. "I feel I have found the Fountain of Youth in my own backyard."

As long as we are able to consciously take a deliberate breath, we can transform our lives. Some have the attitude that it's not worth the trouble at their age. This is simply an old self-limiting belief surfacing, and I ask you to consider this. After all the life experience, training, and knowledge you have acquired, isn't it time you begin to value yourself more? Isn't it time to stop postponing joy?

If you were to have just one day of pure peace and pure love, it would be worth every day you spent to get there. Transformational Breathing is an event not to be missed. Regardless of age or physical condition, you can breathe more deeply, and you deserve to!

"I've released most of my fear of death and made a new, deeper commitment to life. My faith and trust grows everyday," says ReHanna, who lives in California. "My health is so much better now, and I have energy to accomplish my daily activities with greater ease and less stress."

An article concerning a meeting at the National Institute of Aging provides the scientific reasons for this phenomenon. In 1981, *Science News* reported findings from the famous Framingham Heart Study in which a group of 5,200 persons in Massachusetts were observed over a thirty-year span. This study showed that pulmonary function measurement is an indicator of overall health and vigor, and it is literally the primary way to measure potential life span.

Vital lung capacity falls with age—up to seventy-five percent of breathing capacity is lost between the ages of twenty-five and seventy-five (depending on sex and age at the time the test is given) unless steps are taken to arrest or reverse this degeneration. The imminent decline was unmistakable, both in comparing persons of different ages as well as following a group of people as they grow older.

The long term predictive power of vital capacity is what makes it a good candidate as a marker of aging. Long before a person becomes terminally ill, vital capacity can predict life span. It can identify who is going to die ten, twenty, thirty years from now. A person whose vital capacity is low is not going to do as well as someone with a high capacity.

Mechanical engineer and oxygenation researcher Michael Brown has a wonderful way of describing the relationship between aging and oxygenation:

Oxidation is a process of delivering nutrients, digesting our food, and releasing energy. Oxygen cleans up after this process too. Oxygenation could, theoretically, slow the aging process by keeping our cells so clean that they would only wear out very slowly. Instead of aging by toxins, we would only have to contend with the scientifically-admitted effects of cosmic radiation.

As we age, there is a tendency to progressively shut down our breathing mechanism and develop rigidly-set dysfunctional breathing patterns. If we have not done anything to reduce or reverse the accumulation of repressed energy from the stresses of daily living, we eventually shut down energy pathways and begin driving the Life Force out of the body. This catabolic process typically continues until we have completely evicted any remaining spirit out of our physical form. The resulting state is commonly referred to as death.

By practicing Transformational Breathing we reverse the process of unwittingly driving the essence of life from our bodies. We no longer feel like victims at the mercy of either random chance or our ancestors' gene pool. By opening up the breathing mechanism and transforming lifelong repressions, Life Force is invited back into the body, providing a great renewal of energy and youthful vitality.

With many seniors over the years, I have witnessed some amazing responses and recoveries. The following personal stories are offered to demonstrate the wide range of possibilities available to those who are willing to open their minds and use the power of their own breath to rekindle youth and vitality.

One of my most memorable experiences involved a woman I'll call Gloria, whom I also met while teaching at the Deepak

Chopra Center. Gloria was a resident at one of Dr. Chopra's weeklong programs. One of my established clients from Connecticut had told Gloria about her own fascinating experience with Transformational Breathing.

During our initial conversation, I could see how stressed and unhappy Gloria was feeling. She had noticed a lump growing on the back of her neck and was concerned that it might be a recurrence of a previous cancer episode. During our first session, a tremendous amount of emotional trauma surfaced. It was eventually integrated through the breathing, and she ended the session in a state of energized enthusiasm.

Afterward Gloria shared with me that she was astonished at how much more alive she felt and how much old resentment and sorrow had been trailing around behind her. The thing that impressed her most, however, was how quickly it all had moved. The lump on her neck seemed much smaller and had stopped hurting. We then scheduled some additional sessions.

Over the next year, I worked consistently with Gloria as well as with her husband and daughter on a monthly basis. As we continued, she let me know that she did at least a half hour of breathing a day at home and sometimes an hour. At each session, she told me of some of the effects the breathing was having in her life. Her family also commented on how much happier she seemed and how much better her disposition had been since she had started. Besides feeling better than she ever had in her whole life, several physical conditions were improving, not the least of which was the disappearance of that menacing lump.

About four months into the breathing, she mentioned that over the past decade she had suffered from osteoporosis along with a rare blood condition that had required monitoring and certain medications. Her recent medical examination showed that the osteoporosis had leveled off and the blood condition no longer existed.

One of the most interesting comments she made to me was that since she and her husband of more than forty years had been breathing daily, they were now making love every day, which made them both feel younger and more joyful!

Golden Yoga Breathing Program

Similar glowing stories come from Carol Hawk, a certified yoga instructor as well as a certified facilitator and one of our personal growth trainers. Based on the East Coast, she works extensively with groups of seniors who attend her *Golden Yoga*™ program. The class combines gentle stretching and movement with Transformational Breathing and other breathing exercises.

Carol developed this program in 1993, based on her belief that out of 840,000 yoga postures, anyone can do at least some of them. She also knew that everyone breathes. Initially she started with yoga stretching and gradually worked in more and more breathing. She soon realized that it was the *pranayama* (breathing) that was most effective for the seniors.

Terry Lister, who is wheelchair-bound and lives at a home for seniors, says, "The breathing makes me feel more alive. I have more pep."

Since 1993, Carol has completed twenty-four Golden Yoga programs in twelve senior living facilities and worked with over a thousand seniors. The ages of participants have ranged from 55 to 104. Carol stresses the fact that age doesn't necessarily limit one's ability to breathe. In some respects, it is a relatively level playing field.

She has even worked with about a dozen older folks who needed respirators and were still able to participate. Through the breathing exercises, they realized they could still control their breathing by regulating the flow of oxygen during the exercises. This helped them regain some strength and mobility in their lungs and diaphragms, and it also empowered them to be more in control of their lives.

Carol recalls the inception of her program:

The first thing I noticed when I was doing Golden Yoga without stressing the breathing was that my students were tiring so quickly from the postures that I couldn't take a class from beginning to end. This was when I noticed that their breathing was severely shut down.

I then divided the program into three phases. The first phase, called *Breathe Deeply,* introduced them to the simple breathing technique of inhaling slow, deep breaths and exhaling with a sigh. This soon developed into rhythmic breathing with sound and movement, which became phases two and three. Before I knew it, the classes were running a full forty-five minutes to an hour. The students were leaving the class feeling more refreshed than ever! The difference between the first few classes I taught and the revised three-phase classes was astounding.

Typically, Carol begins her classes with gentle stretching movements combined with slower, full-breathing exercises. Then she makes a transition into twenty to forty minutes of Transformational Breathing. For the most part, the students sit in chairs or wheelchairs. "One of the differences in conscious breathing with the seniors is that it is important for them to breathe through the nose instead of the mouth (the standard procedure). This is because they are highly susceptible to pneumonia, and breathing through the nose helps to avoid respiratory infections.

Usually, most of my students come in feeling full of pain, anxiety, and depression. After about ten breaths, their eyes begin to open wider, they become more alert and move more easily. I see smiles and other signs of happiness. They start with a low, dead, zombie-like energy. After the breathing, color comes to their cheeks and they're tapping their feet and laughing a lot. Many of them actually get up from their wheelchairs and push them around. They even begin to touch and relate to each other in a different way. It's very rewarding for me just to watch this!

According to participant Hilda Adams, "It took away my pain and it helps me to relax." Continues Carol:

> *Many older seniors experience a seemingly permanent tightening and drawing up of the arms and hands. A similar temporary phenomenon, called 'tetany,' sometimes happens in Transformational Breathing sessions; tetany usually indicates stored tension and fear. While the integration is occurring, the hands and arms feel temporarily paralyzed. As the breathing continues to work its magic, the tension releases, leaving the limbs more relaxed than ever.*

It amazed me to see that many older people have actually become stuck in that pattern of fear and stress, so much that it becomes a continuous way of being. Emotionally, too, they are stuck in a fear-response pattern (they respond fearfully to any potentially stressful situation, which ensures that it becomes stress)."

As they continue with the breathing, the chronic loss of motion in their arms begins to dissipate and they relax; some have even experienced total recovery—their arms and legs became supple and relaxed again. The breathing helps them move out of the stress response to life and into a relaxation response instead. I've notice corresponding changes in their behavior as well.

Another wonderfully rewarding thing is that, in my ongoing groups of a year or more, because the students associate me with activities that help them feel good, they go into what I call the 'elation' response whenever they see me. They automatically start breathing more deeply and become very elated as soon as I come into view. This certainly adds to my own joy too!

Ray Thomas reports, "My blood pressure has gone down fifteen points since I started doing the breathing."

And Miss Jimmy Ewell says, "The breathing makes me feel happier and more alive."

But the healing for seniors has gone even deeper than this. Many of the East Coast facilities Carol worked at began calling her in to assist with anxiety- and panic-control when all else had failed.

"I would simply get as close as possible to the person experiencing the attack, demonstrate the Transformational Breath and coach them into breathing with me. Before too long, the patient would begin to relax and feel better. It worked every time."

There were also times when she was called in to help control symptoms of Parkinson's disease. After a few minutes of Transformational Breathing, the uncontrollable shaking would decrease or subside for longer periods of time.

Carol says that the seniors love to make loud, clear sounds during sessions. "We do it a lot; it picks them right up. It clears all those years of holding back expression and not being heard. It has been so sweet to see how much they love to be heard and touched, and what a nice opportunity there is to touch them during the breathing."

Another of Carol's students, Ruby Lee Anson says, "The breathing makes me feel younger all the time."

Carol has trained the staff at three nursing homes, which enables them to follow through with the residents between visits. When asked about her most memorable experience with these groups, she shared this story:

I was called in to help an eighty-seven-year-old woman who had been curled up in bed for three days, crying in pain because her stomach hurt so much. As a result, she had become totally withdrawn. I put my hands on her belly and chest and demonstrated the breathing to her. After just a few minutes of breathing, she began to talk and then sobbed and sobbed between breaths for almost an hour. Her condition improved greatly, and later she was able and thrilled to do some breathing exercises on her own.

Modern medical visionaries such as Dr. Deepak Chopra, Dr. Andrew Weil, and Nathaniel Altman put forth in their recent writings the idea that aging and disease are mostly overcome through cellular regeneration. They all agree that the most profound source of cellular nourishment is increased oxygen supply to the system, ideally via the natural method—effective breathing.

Cells replace themselves in 30- to 90-day cycles, and the primary ingredients for healthy cell structure are oxygen and carbon dioxide. Even without this information, anyone who chooses to look can easily see that the key to youthful, healthy living is found in the potential of our own breathing.

*"Happy and aligned are those
who find their homes in the breathing;
to them belong the inner kingdom
and queendom of heaven."*

Aramaic words of Jesus
Prayers of the Cosmos

Breathing into the
Final Transition

Over the years, I have assisted a number of people who were ready to leave this world in making the transition more easily and joyfully. I have learned that even the fear and resistance that often accompany the ultimate surrender can be transformed through conscious breathing.

Holding on to anything in life is demonstrated in our breathing—usually by a tightening of the solar plexus as we exhale. Death represents the final letting go. Being coached to breathe into the solar plexus assists in retraining the muscles to relax. Eventually, the pattern of holding on is integrated so that one can surrender more easily in all areas of life and, finally, in passing.

My most meaningful experience along these lines was the transition of my own mother over a decade ago. She had been seriously ill with thyroid cancer for six months and was in such discomfort, from the intense chemotherapy, that she had not been open to Transformational Breathing during her illness. After her third hospitalization she was released to us—weighing only ninety-two pounds—so she could die more comfortably at home. She was in continuous pain and there was a constant look of terror in her eyes.

On a bright Monday morning in mid-June, I was sitting at her bedside when she suddenly went from a semi-conscious state into doing conscious connected breathing. She just started breathing the way I had prayed she would throughout her entire illness.

I put down my book and began to synchronize my breath with hers. Her eyes opened wide and the window to her soul connected fully with mine. It was a reassurance that she was consciously using the breath to help herself into the next phase of her journey.

We continued to breathe together in unison for about a half hour. At several points, she stopped breathing entirely for a minute or two. I wondered if she was gone. But her breathing resumed and just like in a breathing session, she looked more and more peaceful each time she came back.

In one poignant moment, she opened her eyes and turned them back behind her, peering into thin air with a strong sense of recognition and excitement. I was surprised at the words that came out of my mouth. "It's Daddy—he's here, isn't he?"

My father had passed away eleven months prior. She nodded yes, and tears filled my eyes. The room then filled with an incredible energetic presence. The only thing I had ever felt similar to this was the energy at the birth of my children. It was a feeling of intense joy and grace. The entire apartment seemed to be filled with very bright light. I sensed that she was very close to leaving and, to my surprise, this felt very beautiful.

She took another twelve breaths and then stopped. Then one more breath, a perfect relaxed sigh, and it was over. I experienced a tremendous sense of peace and freedom—a deep inner knowing that she was finally liberated from the body that no longer served her. She was happy and free again.

What happened next shocked me. Instead of feeling loss or sadness, I only felt enormous joy and liberation. And I somehow knew that I was feeling what my mother was feeling. I also felt quite blessed to have shared those precious moments with her. What a gift she had given me after all her months of pain and suffering. She gave me the gift of knowing that the transition of death could be just as exquisite an experience as the transition into life.

Much earlier in life I had learned about the joy of giving birth when able to breathe, relax, and allow it to happen. Now, this same breathing had enabled my mother to be delivered into another dimension, together with me on one side and Dad on the other.

Since this moving experience, I have had the extraordinary opportunity to help a number of others, with the assistance of Transformational Breathing—through their own unique transitions,. I have also had the opportunity to train a number of hospice workers in supporting their clients in finding a more peaceful way Home.

As much as Transformational Breathing can turn a potentially devastating event, such as the death of my own mother, into an experience of grace and wonder at the beauty of life, my preference would be that she had lived much longer. I believe that the breathing could have made it possible if embraced earlier. I'm left here to encourage you to breathe and live as fully as you possibly can before that final inspiration leaves your body and your family behind.

"Transformational Breathing is a miracle to yourself that sits right in front of you. The breath has brought me to a higher consciousness which has helped me through depression, attempted suicide, and daily living as an adolescent."

Carolyne LaCerte, age 14

Psychotherapy,
Prozac, or Breathing

Dr. Henry Smith Rohrberg of Cape Cod, Massachusetts, was a prominent psychotherapist who completed the Transformational Breathing facilitation training some years ago. He had been practicing traditional psychotherapy for more than twenty years when he began working with Transformational Breathing. Dr. Rohrberg was astounded at how quickly so many of his patients' issues were resolved through the breath. He has repeatedly stated that "one Transformational Breathing session can provide the equivalent of two years of traditional therapy."

Traditional psychotherapy works primarily with the conscious mind, reviewing and analyzing dysfunctional patterns and attempting to resolve past issues verbally. Like Transformational Breathing, it aims to liberate the mind from self-created limitations based on past life experiences. It strives to eliminate or alter beliefs and assumptions that have become detrimental to one's personal evolution.

It is obvious, however, that some of the deepest beliefs and behaviors simply do not change as a result of talk therapy, positive thinking, visualization, affirmations, or any purely conscious techniques. Work on these issues can continue session after session, year after year, because our problems are rooted in soil much deeper than the conscious mind. We need to go to that deepest level in order to transform the cellular energies of certain unconscious, hard-driving patterns.

Throughout his numerous best-selling books, John Bradshaw, world-renowned teacher and therapist in the field of addiction recovery, refers to the effort to access and change emotional problems at their core level as "healing the original causes" of our dysfunctional behavior patterns. These original causes are lodged in the subconscious very early in our development and continue to drive our lives if left unhealed. In many cases, psychological illness ensues and even the most basic of functions are difficult or impossible without drugs.

The number of people taking Prozac or Xanax for depression and anxiety, respectively, is astounding to me. And while these drugs can sometimes provide some immediate relief, even the manufacturers advise that patients not rely on them for more than a couple of years. Unfortunately, drugs can only alleviate symptoms temporarily and, in addition to the damage of direct side effects, the original causes continue to snowball. The repressed material simply must be expressed and dealt with somehow.

In addition to the price paid by the physical, emotional, and spiritual bodies, the cost for these drugs drives many to seek public aid. Others simply suffer further under the additional financial stress. Like all attempts to seek solutions outside ourselves, drugs are usually an incomplete solution at best, and often a no-win proposition.

Fortunately, Transformational Breathing offers a safe, effective, alternative. Through breathwork, many people have been successfully weaned off psychiatric drugs. Elizabeth B., M.S.W., says, "I got off antidepressants and prescription allergy medications within two months of my first Transformational Breathing session."

Few therapeutic techniques work effectively at the level of the subconscious mind. Hypnosis can help us access the subconscious to reprogram beliefs with positive affirmations, but unless practitioners address clients' repressed material, it remains in our psyche, continuing to drive our behavior. Transformational Breathing goes to the energetic core of the problem and shifts it to a higher-frequency state, thereby changing the negative patterns and their results in our lives.

I am not saying that Transformational Breathing can or should replace psychotherapy. It is important that we understand and deal with our life issues at the level of the conscious mind. It is also important to go deeper, where we can use the cleansing power of the breath to root out the energetic bases of those problems.

The following section offers stories from just a few of the many mental health professionals who have been certified and use Transformational Breathing in their practices with clients and patients.

A Residential Psychiatric Treatment Facility

Kevin Makarewicz, M.A., is the former head of the expressive therapy program at Well Spring, a psychiatric residential treatment facility for adults and adolescents located in Bethlehem, Connecticut. After completing the Transformational Breathing professional training, he incorporated breath sessions into the treatment plans of his clients and patients several years ago. He saw some impressive results.

"One of the most important benefits is that it gives people a way to contact their healthy energy. By breaking through the defenses of the body and restoring vitality, the breathing moves through physical, psychological, and emotional issues to get to a person's healthy core," he says.

Kevin worked with about thirty people of both sexes and various ages who were experiencing chronic depression. After ten to twelve sessions, each responded to Transformational Breathing in a positive way. His observation was that those who put the most effort into the sessions improved the most. Symptoms always improved, and in some cases they got significantly better or were completely eliminated.

Kevin worked with a number of dysfunctional family situations. In every case, he saw both parents and children become more self-empowered through the breathing. "They also began relating to each other in more positive, loving ways. The breathing assisted them in gaining clarity on personal issues and helped them not to confuse their personal problems with family dynamics," he said.

In cases involving symptoms of acute anxiety, Kevin found that Transformational Breathing helped significantly. "In these cases, most patients gained the ability to use the breathing on their own to monitor and resolve their states of anxiety."

Patients suffering from PTSD (Post-Traumatic Stress Disorder) also responded very favorably. Kevin noticed that these patients tended to "go into a traumatic flash, then breathe through it, and eventually come out and be more relaxed and present."

Comparing the benefits of this breathing technique with traditional psychotherapy, Kevin says, "Breathwork is more holistic. It accesses the whole person, as opposed to talk therapy, which just focuses on the mind. Transformational Breathing is a way to get at what is going on in someone's life and activate them into a process that goes far beyond verbal therapy. What I have seen over and over again is that the breathing gives people who feel despair and hopelessness the experience of hope and aliveness."

Boston Doctor Has Great Success

Since 1994, Dr. Abraham Sussman, a licensed clinical psychologist, has been treating patients with Transformational Breathing as part of his private practice in Boston, Massachusetts. Using this technique for a number of conditions, he has seen many breakthroughs in his clients.

Dr. Sussman reports good responses from people who are "not alert to the vitality of themselves and who are basically underenergized and seem to be living too much in their heads." Clinical Depression is one of the most common diagnoses that come under this description.

He believes that Transformational Breathing gives such people an experience of their own inner flow and vitality. He observed that energy and optimism increase as a result. "The advantage that Transformational Breathing adds to relational therapy is that it provides us with an energetic, active, vital experience of ourselves. It promotes the awakening of more levels of a human being. It can then open us up to our inner world. Often when we are having a deeper experience of ourselves, we push through many layers of emotion. This allows us to come to terms with various aspects of ourselves and to integrate what comes up."

People who are over concerned with how others see them also respond well. Dr. Sussman describes these people as being too "otherly" oriented. "After experiencing breathing sessions, they found a good reference point for accessing their own inner experience. This helped them develop an independent ability to self-evaluate and get in touch with their own inner world."

For dissociative people—those withdrawn into an overactive inner world—Transformational Breathing"was effective in a safe, well-established relationship, where risks were acknowledged." Within that framework, he determined that "the breath therapy created peace, balance, and adjustment."

Dr. Sussman says that conditions of fear and anxiety are most successfully treated with breathing when located somatically (in the body). "The breathing provides individuals with the experience of being alone, then finding self. This helps fears to diminish," he said. "I see Transformational Breathing as a valuable tool in psychotherapy."

A Wide Range of Applications

Samvedam Randles is a Diplomat Psychologist, L.M.H.C., and a Reichian therapist with additional training and experience in Postural Integration. Co-founder of the Body Oriented Center for Psychotherapy in Somerville, Massachusetts, she has worked extensively with Transformational Breathing personally, with family members, and in her professional practice.

Samvedam offers monthly breathing classes and weekend intensives called "The Inner Art of Breathing." She has guided more than 2,500 people in group and individual sessions toward extraordinary transformation and recovery. She reflects that a defining moment in her life was when she was able to use the breath in assisting her mother's transition from a painful terminal illness into heavenly peace.

Samvedam's overall enthusiasm for using Transformational Breathing in her work comes through loud and clear:

I love it. I enjoy the energetic changes it brings about—major things happen on that level. We do not get stuck on the mental levels, as it clues people in, right away, about what is going on in the deeper levels. I breathe with everyone who is ready to do it. Some clients want to talk, initially, and then move into it.

For example, there is some controversy over using Transformational Breathing with trauma survivors, because it can put them back in the midst of the past traumatic experiences. I have found, however, that they need to learn to go on another track so as not to repeat these patterns of abuse. The therapist should also be skilled in working with someone with a traumatic history. We need to be able to hang in there with them, so they do not repeat similar patterns. Because things can move very rapidly, clients can sabotage results if they feel they are moving too quickly. A certain level of trust needs to be developed.

Samvedam finds Transformational Breathing sessions very effective for clients with depression—"Breathing helps them feel again and move past the debilitation of depression"—and she obtains good results with clients who want to stop overeating and smoking.

She also incorporates breathwork in treating Multiple Personality Disorder and Post Traumatic Stress Disorder. "These individuals commonly report having 'high' experiences, such as seeing lights, feeling profound peace, and experiencing joy on a consistent basis."

In Samvedam's experience, Transformational Breathing has been most effective in cases of generalized anxiety disorder (panic attacks). "It first helps people understand what frightened them or made them anxious in the first place. Then it gives them a way to monitor and resolve these feelings."

She recalls a client in her seventies who had panic attacks and was unable to feel emotions. She had been treated by five psychiatrists with no success. After a series of breathing sessions, she experienced great improvement. Panic attacks were far less frequent and had become manageable with breathing exercises.

She also reported connecting with her feelings, which she had not been able to do for as long as she could remember.

Samvedam says that, since incorporating breath techniques, her work is more enjoyable and rewarding. Her clients are more present and move through issues more quickly. "Everything we need to accomplish the goals that we set up becomes so much more accessible."

Multiple Personalities Integrate

Transformational Breathing is very powerful in aligning aspects of personality and self that have been lost, feared, or disowned. It allows us to embrace and integrate all aspects of our nature, including what Jung calls our shadow self. The process becomes a *soul retrieval* of sorts. Even though the soul itself never really gets lost, we do separate "unacceptable" aspects of our personality from our conscious self. The integrative action of Transformational Breathing brings these aspects into awareness and allows us the opportunity to embrace once-rejected experiences, accept, forgive, and bring home the lost, unhealed parts of ourselves.

Many cases of Multiple Personality Disorder involve fragmented aspects of the personality that have no grounded way of reunifying with the whole. Sometimes referred to in laymen's terms as split personality, the most famous case of MPD was written about extensively by Flora Rheta Schreiber in her groundbreaking book, *Sybil.*

I have witnessed many amazing and lasting improvements in people who suffered with MPD. Even people with severe psychological conditions have responded dramatically to Transformational Breathing. One example was Susan, a woman in her early forties, who had been diagnosed with Multiple Personality Disorder. The medical and psychiatric communities had given up on treating Susan's condition. They told her she would have to live with her symptoms and manage the best she could. She was unable to work, had recently gained over fifty pounds, and was in an almost constant state of feeling overwhelmed. The vast array of consequences, brought on by the many different personalities living within and expressing through her, had created an unbearable chaos in her life. Earlier in life, she had maintained a professional career for more than ten years. But she was increasingly experiencing the uncontrollable presence of other personalities, and at some of the most inappropriate times.

It took Susan several meetings to get to the point where she was able to relax and trust enough to do the breathing. When we began her series of sessions, the mixture of beings inside Susan became apparent in her breathing. It was one of the most interesting breathing patterns I had ever seen, popping up in lots of areas of the respiratory system at once. The pattern would be impossible to duplicate deliberately.

During one of her initial sessions, Susan went back to a time when she was sixteen. She became terrified as she remembered being hypnotized without her full consent and being taken advantage of sexually while in the hypnotic trance. This had apparently triggered a major split in her personality and consciousness, and was apparently the underlying cause of her multiple personalities. As she continued to breathe, the fear moved through her and gradually resolved.

Susan continued to come for regular breath sessions over a six-month period. As more and more fragmented aspects of her self surfaced, we worked with each of them. I witnessed as they integrated into the primary conscious identity called Susan. After much emotional healing, she was finally able to forgive the young man who had violated her.

Within a year, the symptoms that had been plaguing her for many years were just a memory. She was weaned off the medications and began to feel and act like one very interesting multifaceted personality once again. By the end of the second year, Susan had gained enough confidence to take the Transformational Breathing facilitator training. She returned to school and now works happily as a breath therapist and counselor.

Freedom from Antidepressants

During a very stressful period in John's life, his physician had prescribed antidepressants as a short-term measure. Six years later, still on medication, John was also seeking other methods of dealing with stress and emotions; the antidepressants were adversely affecting the quality of his life, spoiling his sex life with his wife, and making him feel like a "walking zombie, not really dead or alive."

John remembered once having ambitions and goals for his life, but he was running out of steam and motivation, and hope was wearing thin.

As we began breath sessions, John was able to get in touch with some early childhood trauma and the intense grief of losing one of his parents. It was during that difficult period that he had begun fighting off or stuffing down the emotions associated with those events.

Within the safety of a guided breath session, he found the inner strength and courage to finally confront those memories and feelings. Allowing them to surface, he let himself feel the pain fully, finally expressing it and therefore setting it free. Once we stop banishing our feelings or imprisoning them in the dungeons of our soul, we find that the actual experience is not nearly as painful as the imagined one.

After three sessions, John intuitively knew he no longer needed medication. The buried feelings, which had created so much of his stress and anxiety, were no longer present. He worked with his doctor and, over a period of a few months, was able to eliminate the antidepressants. He has not felt a need to resume them, saying he feels better than ever.

A similar situation occurred with a woman named Amy, a successful interior decorator, who had been on antidepressants for three years, yet still felt a tremendous amount of anxiety. Her relationships were suffering and she felt paranoid about many of her friends. She described herself as feeling "numb to life and excitement."

In her breathing sessions, Amy worked through a lot of old emotions, mostly extreme terror. It was astounding to me how the medication could have kept such intense feelings at bay for so long. I have noticed that repressed feelings tend to pile up even faster when continuously subdued through the artificial means of medication. With prescriptions, as with self-medication, there is no true resolution of emotions; drugs merely postpone dealing with feelings.

By Amy's sixth session, she had integrated a tremendous amount of fear, terror, and resistance. Her relationships were improving, and the paranoid feelings were gone. She related to me that she was feeling more peaceful than ever before and experiencing a new level of confidence. Over the next few months, she worked with her therapist and was soon completely off antidepressants.

What I have consistently seen in working with people who are taking mood-altering drugs is that the breathing provides both an opportunity to free oneself from the medicine and to heal the feelings that initiated the need for the medication. Transformational Breathing brings them up into the light of day and then quickly and safely transforms them into creative energy.

Long-Term Depression

Angie, a woman in her early fifties, had been plagued with feelings of gloom and despair for the past three years. She had been into holistic healing for many years and had tried every technique she knew to rid herself of these feelings. Nothing gave her the relief she sought. The harder she tried to get rid of the depression, the more frustrated and depressed she became at her inability to resolve it. When she came for her first session she shared with me that she had given up hope of ever conquering these feelings, but she was willing to try anything that might make even the slightest difference in how she felt.

Angie's first session was very powerful. She cried and expressed a lot of repressed trauma and emotion. After the session she felt so light and clear that she broke down in tears of joy for the new sense of hope she felt. She continued doing sessions and experienced such a change in her life that she decided to take the

TBF Personal and Professional Training. Soon after she finished the program, she quit her cumbersome job and has found incredible joy and fulfillment in her new life and job. Angie hardly remembers the despair and hopelessness that she once felt.

Anxiety Attacks

Abandoned by her parents and raised by her grandmother, Diane experienced a good deal of abuse throughout her life. In her late forties, she was experiencing many painful physical symptoms, primarily in the intestinal and stomach areas. After many years of various medications and a half dozen surgeries, she was still experiencing anxiety and listlessness.

When I started working with Diane, she was taking at least three prescription medicines, which kept her mind in a state of confusion. We started doing Transformational Breathing sessions and she noticed a difference right away.

I was not surprised to find that she was not breathing into the lower respiratory system. As soon as she started to breathe into the stomach and abdomen, a Pandora's box of traumatic and fearful emotions from childhood surfaced and quickly resolved. One of her major past traumas involved the fact that she had never really grieved the loss of her grandmother, the woman who had raised her.

As she continued with regular breathing sessions, Diane continued to feel better and better. She graduated from a liquid diet to being able to keep down solid food. With the help of her physician, she began to wean herself off most of her medications. She was now able to stop and do some connected-breathing exercises whenever she felt anxiety coming on. Consequently, her panic attacks decreased in frequency and intensity

Manic Depression or Bipolar Disorder

Working with symptoms of manic depression has also been amazingly beneficial. One such experience involved Tom, a young man who, at nineteen, had begun having what his family called mental breakdowns. Tom would lose all sense of identity during a breakdown and behave in extremely bizarre ways. He appeared to be hallucinating and carrying on as though he was other people in other times. Initially diagnosed as schizophrenic, after three hospitalizations, he was rediagnosed as bipolar.

Bipolar Disorder is the more popular medical term for manic depression which is characterized by extreme changes in mood and behavior, typically shifting between periods of severe depression and manic activity.

Tom and his wife had been informed that there was no cure for his condition, but that the episodes could be controlled by taking Lithium. The prescription left him feeling groggy, drugged, and unable to perform many of the athletic activities he had once enjoyed.

We began doing breath therapy after his third hospitalization. He had already been on Lithium for almost a full year. During the sessions, we went through what I would call dissociative personality expression in which he expressed aspects of personality that he had disowned and repressed in the subconscious. The breathing brought these parts of the psyche into consciousness to be healed and integrated into his overall personality. I also witnessed a good deal of detoxification from all the drugs in his system.

After our sessions, Tom began feeling more lively, clear, and focused, and soon realized that he needed to stay away from substances such as alcohol and marijuana, which aggravated his condition. He presently maintains a small dosage of lithium, and has not experienced any breakdowns since beginning breath sessions. In fact, Tom was so encouraged by the results from the breathing that he took the Facilitator Training and began sharing it with others.

Suicidal Tendencies

Jeremy was a young man in his early twenties who described himself as "having always been in pain." The way he dealt with his pain was to hurt himself. When I met Jeremy, his self-abuse was escalating, his most recent self-assault resulting in major physical injuries and hospitalization. Prompted by a family member, Jeremy agreed to do some Transformational Breathing. After his first session, he felt very good for several days and had no thoughts of hurting himself. After the second session, a lot of old emotions surfaced and he found himself feeling a great deal of emotional freedom. The third session left him with feelings of total peace and serenity, unlike any he had ever experienced. He continues to use Transformational Breathing daily to keep progressing and feeling good about himself and his life.

Eating Disorder

Marcia was a woman in her mid-thirties who had experienced eating disorders most of her life and was at least sixty pounds overweight when she began Transformational Breathing. Her pattern was to starve herself, then binge, then make herself regurgitate.

Marcia confessed that she was always feeling deprived or guilty about food—either hating her eating or hating herself. She was caught in a vicious cycle and had tried every diet and cure she came across. Some worked for a while, but, little by little, her old habits would creep back in and she would become more dysfunctional and feel more ashamed than ever.

Marcia made an appointment with me soon after hearing that I had lost thirty pounds after starting Transformational Breathing.

One of the first realizations that came up for Marcia in her session was how little she was nurtured as a child and how she took to eating as a form of self-caring. In the breathing session, she came to realize that there were healthier ways to nurture herself, ways that would allow her to live in harmony with herself and with life. In her second session, she received insights into altering her eating habits and food choices that would work better for her. To her surprise, she found it easy to make those changes. Soon she was eating, feeling, and looking much better. After one year of consistent breath sessions, Marcia was forty pounds lighter and no longer binging and purging.

"Resisting corruption,
possessing integrity
are those whose breath
forms a luminous sphere:
they hear the Universal Word
and feel the earth's power
to accomplish it
through their own hands."

Aramaic words of Jesus
Prayers of the Cosmos

Unlocking the Inner Prisoner

Since 1970, the number of people incarcerated in United States federal prisons has increased 500%. Think about that fact. In 1998, there were five times as many people in prisons as there were just thirty years ago. And the shocking part is that nearly 59% of sentenced prisoners are serving time for drug offenses, compared with only 16.3% drug offenders in 1970 (Federal Bureau of Prisons Statistics). Consider the enormous waste of talent, energy, and money that this fact represents!

If you've never been in prison you may not think about this often, but consider the amount of your tax dollars spent on this problem. The average cost per incarcerated individual is over $20,000 per year (!), yet all too often the only result is more problems: at least 47% of those released from prison return within three years. Obviously, our current system is only making matters worse.

We have only begun to explore the extensive possibilities of using the breath in criminal rehabilitation programs in prisons, and the results have been inspiring. Several short-term programs featuring Transformational Breathing have been completed in maximum and minimum-security prisons. Plans are underway to implement a more in-depth long-term program, which will serve as a model for prisons everywhere.

Circumstances are rare in which strong motivation to make internal change is accompanied by an abundance of time for the individual to focus on doing so. While many of us are faced with time restraints that compete with the desire to focus on our own healing, inmates are in the midst of what could become an ideal formula for healing and transformation. They have plenty of time to reflect on their lives, and once that glimmer of hope is experienced in their first breath session, most inmates gain a great deal of motivation.

Destructive patterns and deep wounds in the subconscious mind typically underlie the reasons for serious criminal behavior. Hiding deep within the psyche, these patterns and the resulting pain and tension are ultimately expressed in the form of violence or other offensive actions. Hurtful behavior is seldom driven by careful, conscious thought, but rather by subconscious patterns that overpower our innate desire to love and be loved. The only way to eliminate the drive to react based on our woundedness, is to heal the wounds.

Giving tougher sentences and making more laws obviously does not help the situation. If it did, the United States would not have the highest incarceration rate in the world. The current correction system does not correct anything. It actually reinforces the hideous fears and beliefs that lead to criminal behavior in the first place.

If we do not provide inmates the opportunity to heal their wounds and gain a new perspective on their own potential, they will continue destructive behaviors that hurt all of us in the long run. As we all become prisoners to a system that is self-perpetuating, it will continue to grow, demanding more fearful thoughts and financial sacrifice from you and me.

For Transformational Breathing programs, the toughest challenge has been gaining access to some of those dark, closed-off institutions. Most of what we have done to date has been on a volunteer basis.

Cynthia Van Savage has been a dedicated leader in the process of opening the doors to prisoner rehabilitation. A professional performer and a Certified Transformational Breathing Facilitator, her caring and selfless work in the prison system began as a result of sharing her own profound transformation from childhood abuse to a life of recovery, hope, and joy.

Throughout her twenties and beyond, Cynthia struggled with substance abuse. During the last few of those years, fear filled her life. She became agoraphobic, was plagued with panic attacks, and had difficulty breathing due to anxiety.

She eventually began reading and meditating to develop self-awareness. At the age of thirty-four, Cynthia stopped drinking. When incest memories began to surface a few years later, the anxiety and panic returned. Transformational Breathing was a primary tool she used to overcome the devastating fear.

As part of her own healing process, Cynthia created a one-woman musical, entitled *Trees of Hope: A Celebration of Life*. In sharing the show, she felt drawn to audiences who were aware of the need for therapeutic relief, and the strongest response came from prisons. Both male and female inmates were permitted to come to the theatre on furlough to see *Trees of Hope*. Because their response was so open and enthusiastic, she asked permission to run an experimental program with the men.

Since 1995, Cynthia has developed and presented Self-Empowerment Training programs in several correctional facilities to a variety of populations. A number of communication techniques and self-esteem exercises were used, however the core of the program was Transformational Breathing.

Here she describes her first twelve-week program, held at Garner Correctional Institute in Newtown, Connecticut:

> *The first group consisted of twenty men. Initially, I felt apprehensive about giving them a full breath session. In the first three meetings, we did some Kundalini Yoga breathing exercises. The men really got into it.*
>
> *In the fourth class, I felt a lot of anger and tension in the room. I knew this was the perfect time to forge ahead with a full session. I did a silent prayer and we proceeded. We started with about thirty minutes of movement and breathing. Then the men sat in their chairs and continued with the full, circular Transformational Breath. I was even allowed to dim the lights, which is normally forbidden in that setting. It was difficult for many men to even close their eyes while in a roomful of other inmates. I believe*

that, for many of them, it would take a long time to break the walls that were once erected to protect their vulnerability. Yet I witnessed the breathing process open up and transform many of them. After the full twelve-week program, the results were awesome.

One inmate said, "It makes me more relaxed and aware of the emotions and feelings towards other people. More respect of inmates in the group. I find myself more aware of the problem inside of me and can even talk about my feelings and emotions."

Another reported, "The breathing helps me stay out of trouble. I used to go off easily. Now I'm relaxed and don't care what people do. I sleep better because I am not worrying. I have fourteen years in a 120-year sentence, and I'm not as frustrated with my situation. I want to see this as a regular program."

"There are many stories I could share," says Cynthia, "but the biggest reward for me is sharing the feeling of unconditional love, which so many of the inmates reported experiencing for the very first time. I attribute this directly to the breathing. I was amazed to see how far the breath could take even the most disenfranchised of inmates. Many of the men experienced profound positive changes in their attitudes and behavior."

The following comments speak for themselves:

One inmate, who had been notorious for getting in fights, said, "It's been a long time since I wanted to punch someone. I was in a confrontation and got so mad all I wanted to do was punch him. I walked away instead. I realized afterwards it was because I had started the breathing we do in class."

Another man had been very angry at the start of the program because of some childhood abuse remembered in a session. He reported, "I have been using the breathing every morning in the kitchen where I work, and I am not reacting to people and their attitudes anymore." He was also grateful for learning how to avoid solitary confinement: "I was recently in an argument with a correctional officer and he got me very upset. I went to my cell and did some deep breathing, and all of a sudden I felt better."

Cynthia explains this shift in self-control as a result of self-acceptance that grows out of the breathing experience:

> *Fear of our own feelings drives us to give away our power to others. When I react to your attacks, I am giving you my power because your actions are instigating mine. Real power comes from within–from not being afraid to acknowledge and honor our own deepest feelings. When I am denying my feelings, I am hurting myself and others can sense it and join in. They can get their hooks in you. When I am accepting my own feelings, I am loving myself and therefore do not need anyone else's acceptance. I have nothing to defend when I am okay with myself.*

Many inmates' comments reflected a new level of self-awareness. One reported, "Since enrolling in this class, I've become spiritually in tune with my inner feelings. I find the program to be of great benefit in my daily life."

Another said, "It has me dealing with my inner self and my emotions. I have the ability to recognize when I'm about to lose control, and I can stop it before it happens."

Yet another inmate reported, "I now know who and what I am, and that I am to blame—only me."

Cynthia often receives confirmation from staff members regarding the inmates' behavioral changes. One afternoon, a counselor pulled her aside and whispered that she was grateful a certain inmate's angry outbursts had ceased. The inmate later wrote on the feedback form offered at the end of the program:

> *You have given me something that no one has ever given me: peace of mind. Before the breathing experience I had in class, I used to drive myself crazy about my father. There were times when I couldn't sleep, eat, or even talk about him. I now know he loves me, and he knows I love him. He told me so. And I haven't been the same since.*

In addition to the psychological benefits, many inmates also reported physical health improvements. "Since I started breathing, I am more understanding in ways of dealing with others. Although I suffer from emphysema, breathing is easier. I feel my lungs to be more relaxed."

An asthma sufferer echoed similar results, "My lungs feel better, and I am breathing better."

Still another reported, "It relaxes me. It takes the rough edges off. No more medications—and it relieves my arthritis pain."

An inmate who had been using the infirmary regularly, due to severe migraine headaches, said, "I use the breathing to stop arguments and to stop my migraines."

These kinds of health benefits are of value not only to the inmates themselves, but to taxpayers as well.

Eventually, Cynthia was given permission to run an extended program; this time using mats in the gym with a mental health counselor present. This was more effective for some of the inmates who had difficulty relaxing while sitting up.

She recalls a middle-aged tough guy - a career criminal - who had been unwilling to close his eyes, in prior sessions, because he was the self-appointed leader of the group. In the gym, however, he pulled a mat into a corner away from the group.

Cynthia recalls, "He laid down, and I was glad to see that he managed to close his eyes. In the fourth gym session, he achieved activation for the first time. He had to leave the class early, and, just as he was getting up, I stumbled while moving from one inmate to another. I was astounded by the expression of genuine concern and compassion beaming from his eyes as he asked if I was okay. I immediately knew that he had had a transformational experience, which he confirmed when asked about his session. It felt like a big milestone."

Cynthia was also given the opportunity to introduce the entire mental health staff to Transformational Breathing. The group session was attended by psychiatrists, counselors, and nurses - most of whom found it difficult to lie on their backs on mats in the prison gym. However, several staff members were able to relax into the breathing, and one therapist had a profound mystical experience and also resolved some childhood issues. After the session, he took about ten minutes to collect himself and think about what had happened. "All that education," he later exclaimed, "and we don't know shit!"

"One day," Cynthia recalls, "the Director of Addiction Services called to tell me what a tremendous change she had seen in one of the men. She couldn't believe the difference in his appearance and his process. He used Transformational Breathing to help resolve a lot of emotions that had troubled him for years. He contacted me after being released from prison, in the beginning of 1998, to say that he felt it was our group experience at Garner that had been the reason for his transformation. After being released, not only did he find gainful employment, but he has also been very active in the AA network, is a responsible father to his children, and has recently begun working with other addicts detoxifying in a rehab center."

The Self-Empowerment Training was also offered at the J.R. Manson Youth Institute, a maximum security facility for men ages sixteen to twenty-one, with similar encouraging responses. Cynthia remembers:

> *One time, during a powerful group session, a young inmate cried out in emotional pain. When he failed to return to the next meeting, I learned from the mental health staff that he had felt humiliated after allowing himself to be so vulnerable. He shared with me privately, however, that the experience had helped him to feel aspects of himself that he had never realized existed.*

At the end of the program, this group presented Cynthia with a certificate they had made. The comments each of them wrote on the back of the certificate reflected how deeply touched they were by the experience, and how they were helped on many levels.

One young man, who had come from a violently abusive childhood, was in prison for a long time for committing a very violent crime. He wrote on the certificate that the group had affected him greatly, and that he would never be the same. He told Cynthia that the changes he experienced in the breathing sessions would last his entire lifetime.

The following letter was sent to the warden by a young man who reported an experience of "breathing into pure light."

> *Dear Warden,*
> *I would like to thank you for allowing me to be a part of the Self-Empowerment Program. It is a unique group. It*

*helped me stop and think about life's pressures, and helps
me realize that it's all bearable. Being incarcerated
sometimes makes me feel like I will never get another
chance to really be somebody because of my past. But
this group helped me realize that I'm still in control of my
life, and that I have the chance to make improvements if I
really want to. I really appreciated this group and all who
got involved voluntarily to help and show they care.*

  Thank you,
  T.G.

Cynthia recalls that after this man's breathing session, "our eyes met and he smiled. It was beautiful to see such love in his smiling eyes. I had always felt that he was the most committed member of the group, but he had held back until that last session. It was very gratifying to see him receive so much in return for what he had put into his healing journey with Transformational Breathing."

Another member of this same group, J.D. was serving a thirteen-year sentence due to his gang involvement at the age of fourteen. He was eighteen-years-old the day he walked into Cynthia's first class at the J.R. Manson facility, with dark sunglasses and a very cool, arrogant attitude. He acted as though he had it all together and was just there to kill time. Cynthia was surprised when he waited until everyone else had left and asked if he could participate. "I told him that he could have as much attitude as he wanted as long as it didn't interfere with anyone else's progress."

After the third class, J.D. got in trouble and was put into isolation for two weeks. Upon returning to class he was noticeably more relaxed. He told Cynthia that while in isolation he had done the breathing every day, sometimes for hours, and cried and cried and cried. He felt sure that the anger he had carried around for so long had dissipated. When the program was discontinued, J.D. also wrote to the warden asking that it be continued. He wrote, "This has been the only [program] to really help me. Other inmates should have the opportunity to be a part of this group because it really works."

This same young man has since dedicated his life to exposing the truth about gangs as best he can from behind the fence. His goal is to help communities to find ways "to influence the kids in a positive way instead of letting the gangs influence them."

Cynthia reflects proudly on an article J.D. wrote imploring society to support young kids in finding power within, so they will not be such easy prey to the lure of gangs. The following is a revealing excerpt:

> *For a young teenager to have so much power is a rush that not many of them can handle without letting it go to their heads. To be able to have someone hurt or even killed is an attraction that most kids cannot resist, especially at the age of fourteen. You see the money, the nice gold, the girls who like that bad-boy attitude, and you want to be a part of it. It's so easy that you can't even believe your eyes. Soon you have those black and gold colors around your neck as a symbol that you are a member of the gang. Nobody could touch, disrespect, hit, or make fun of you without getting their head knocked off.*
>
> *After you do all you have to do to get your colors and you're making money, have girls, and are respected by everyone in your crew, they drop the punch line on you: Once you're in, you can't get out. Then you start getting missions in which you have to beat up or shoot anyone they tell you to. [J.D.'s best friend was killed at the age of fourteen for disobeying the gang leader.]*
>
> *Kids today are killing and dying, and that's nothing to laugh at. Still, no one is doing anything to stop them. The police are arresting them, but that is not working because, for every member they put in jail, there are two to take his place.*

In June of 1998, J.D. wrote to Cynthia happily reporting, "I am still doing the breathing exercises. It has actually become part of my daily routine. And whenever it gets too hectic for me, I do my breathing and help myself relax. Since I've done your group, I have not been to [solitary confinement] once."

As she talks and works with people who are imprisoned by self-destructive behavior, Cynthia's goal is that each person will be able to say and believe, "I have a choice. I don't have to be a product of the past. I can be in the present. I can close the door on crime, violence, and abuse. I can open the door to responsibility, maturity and positive change."

I am truly grateful to Cynthia for her courageous and caring work in this most challenging of environments, and I applaud those inmates who allow themselves to receive and embrace the precious gift that she offers. Needless to say, there is much breathing to be done in prisons, and it will benefit every one of us.

21

Opening to the Infinite

For centuries, great teachers from the Eastern hemisphere have declared the breath to be the key to awaken the infinite possibilities within us. Yogi master Babaji once stated, "The breath is the gateway between the visible and invisible worlds."

In one of his Aramaic prayers, Jesus proclaims, "Blessed are those who are refined in breath; they shall find their ruling principles and ideals guided by God's light."

In the Dead Sea Scrolls, Jesus discusses the sacredness of breathing: "Breathe long and deeply, that the angel of air may be brought within you. I tell you truly, the angel of air shall cast out of your body all uncleanness which defiled it without and within. No man may come before the face of God whom the angel of air lets not pass. Truly all must be born again by air and by truth, for your body breathes the air of the Earthly Mother, and your spirit breathes the truth of the Heavenly Father."

Modern Christian doctrine also refers to Holy Spirit as the Breath of Life.

Recent studies and ancient spiritual principles are in agreement that the unconscious mind is the passageway to the Spiritual realms of existence. This unconscious mind contains all consciousness beyond our usual state of awareness, and our breath is the doorway into that unconscious realm. This unique aspect of the breath–that it can be either a fully conscious or fully unconscious process–allows us to bring these unconscious states into our awareness and harness their incredible power.

For some, Transformational Breathwork begins an amazing mystical journey. In the first two stages, or levels, we evolve as we open our breath and clear the repressed energy in our subconscious. In level three, we continue to expand, connecting more fully with our Spirit. For many, the experience becomes one of spiritual atonement ("at-one-ment") and exploration.

Jeanne Marie, a graduate of the training program, reported this experience during one of her training weekends:

> *Beings of light appeared, surrounding me, holding me, and placing their hands under and over my legs and their arms around my body. They appeared more as light than as bodies—no clear features or extremities—and they seemed to blend into one another. I asked them to come to me at every session and their response was We have been with you since the beginning of time."*
>
> *As the session ended, the beings remained and when I stood up they stood with me. Several people came around me as we began to form a circle, and when the circle was complete, the light beings became the human beings in the circle.*

Witnessing the many inner journeys and mystical experiences participants have taken over the years has indeed been a joy. It never ceases to amaze me how varied and vast those experiences can be. Each and every time, these awakenings seem unique and precious—a reflection of the infinite possibilities of life.

In the following story, Dennis Straub describes an experience he had during his very first Transformational Breathing Experience:

> *I had heard a little about Transformational Breathing; however, I never could have imagined the gift in store for me that day: time with my ten-year-old daughter, Lauren, who had passed away just one year earlier.*
>
> *Music was playing as I lay down and began the connected breathing. Soon I began receiving powerful images. I experienced moving through a series of exciting journeys, and with each adventure there were obstacles to*

overcome to get to my final destination.

Eventually, I was told I had completed my journeys and would now be meeting with my daughter, Lauren. I felt the weight of her body sitting across my stomach, as she had often done, and could see her looking down at me, smiling and crying. The look in her eyes was of true love, and happiness that I had been her father. At first, all we could do was look deep into each other's eyes.

Later I was able to share with her the one question that had haunted me since the time of her passing. "Why did you leave, Lauren? I have so missed the experience of watching you grow up. I felt cheated out of the opportunity to attend a Daddy Daughter Dance with you." Her response was that anyone could attend the Daddy Daughter Dance, but what we had together was the Dance of Life.

Next we were in a huge ballroom filled with music played by Angels in an orchestra section to the side. The ceiling of the ballroom seemed to be made of pearl, like the inside of a seashell. Lauren was wearing a light blue formal gown. Her blonde, naturally curly hair flowed halfway down her back, the way it had been before the chemotherapy treatments. The whole ballroom was ours! We danced, talked, and, looking deep into each other's eyes, communicated without words at a much higher level.

As the parent of a child who passed early, I just can't express in words how healing and powerful Transformational Breathing has been for my grieving process. Through the breath sessions, my questions were answered, I found peace, and I felt what it was like to be the father of a High and Powerful Angel who had come to Earth and completed her mission in ten short years. Just being together again, even for a short while, was indescribably precious to me.

Henry Orion, of North Carolina, recounts this story of his first meeting with his Native American self, while practicing Transformational Breathing:

My wife, Janet, and I are fortunate to have access to a magnificent untouched wilderness secluded in the mountains of western North Carolina. On one extraordinarily beautiful evening there, while engaged in fully activated Transformational Breathing, I spontaneously experienced a profound spiritual connection to my Native American spirit guides.

After one powerfully long inhalation, I felt the presence of a very ancient, wise, spiritual elder descend from the heavens. I was overwhelmed with awe and inspiration. A part of me ascended with this being and I was led to a group of ten to twelve Native American elders assembled in a circle. As I approached the council, part of the circle opened. There was a huge fire in the center. As I then observed more closely, these council members were actually part of the center flame of intense bright white light. There was no separation between their bodies and the fire. They were not burning themselves. They were inherently part of this divine energy. An overwhelming sense of humility developed within me. As my body bowed down, I felt tremendously grateful to be invited into their divine presence.

My breathing continued and I felt totally open to receiving whatever wisdom and deeper appreciation these magnificent beings could give me. They shared with me a profound understanding of the Native American phrase "Mitakuye Oyasin," *which translates to "All My Relations."* This was spoken to me in a dialect that I did not understand but was able to experience directly through my body. Extraordinary visual images of every form of life in and on the earth moved through me, and I felt the spiritual energy of every animal, plant, mineral, insect, fish, lake, stream, and ocean of the world flow up through me into the heavens. Spontaneously, I started to chant in words that sounded like a Native American language. I felt my physical body transform into a young Native American brave. I experienced amazing strength. Janet later told me that she perceived long braids of hair fall across my chest.

Looking skyward, I again became aware of the presence of that first spiritual elder. His face descended to me on a ball of brilliant light with one final powerful inhalation. I felt older, wiser and ready to pass on my heightened awareness and understanding of "Mitakuye Oyasin." *Very gradually my body fell to the ground next to Janet as I continued to chant gently the phrases given to me in this ceremony of Spirit and profound understanding. This connection to Spirit remains with Janet and me forever.*

Experiences of the Divine in my own sessions occur primarily as ecstatic feelings and visions of light. Many people interact with angels and spiritual teachers. Some go into pure energetic states where they experience themselves as various expressions of pure energy. It is quite difficult to describe what many have called the *indefinable* levels of reality that demonstrate the unlimited aspects of existence and our truest nature. It is common to experience realms filled with such loving energies that we can only weep with joy.

Another such experience:

"Transformational Breathing has truly, truly transformed my life at every level, mental, emotional, spiritual, physical. It has transformed all my relationships, especially with myself. It has helped me to move into the space of being Spirit and truly knowing from within myself, I am that, and extend it to all that is. *I am in touch with more joy now than I ever thought possible, and more love than I ever dreamed. I now embrace life, all of it, in all forms. I don't need love because I* am *love. This training has delivered far more than I ever could have imagined. There are no words to adequately express it."*

I invite you to step forward to experience and embrace this form of breath therapy as many thousands have. You will surely transform your life from one of struggle and pain to one of ease and joy. You will become a natural source of energy as abundant as the Sun. You will lead the way—a beacon in the darkness lighting the flames of Spirit within.

*"Judith Kravitz is the most impressive teacher
of breathwork I have ever encountered in
both the East and the West.
Her techniques have the power
to lead one to have a direct experience
of liberation on many levels.
You may call it a short cut to enlightenment."*

Tulku Rimpoche Thubten,
Tibetan Buddhist Lama

Appendix A
Breath Analysis Checklist

Following is a summarized list of key areas of the body, what they represent and how they relate to the breath.

Mouth and jaw:

Closing the mouth as we exhale is a way of holding on to toxic negativity (repressed energy and feelings). A tight or clenched jaw is one of the most powerful ways to control and hold down expression; it indicates repression of ourselves and our feelings, especially of strong feelings such as grief and anger.

Affirmations: I accept my good. I release all my fear and anger. It is safe to express my feelings. I allow myself to receive joy.

Throat

This area is related to self-expression. Clenched throat muscles indicate the inability to express oneself. It is likely that people exhibiting this pattern were not permitted as children to express who they are, and perhaps they are still not permitting themselves to do so. They may gag, cough, or choke back their feelings which strive to be released. This inner conflict creates further stress. Being able to breathe with ease in this area can result in a greater ability to express oneself as well as an improved sense of freedom and ease.

Affirmations: It is easy to breathe. It is safe to express myself fully. My expression is free and clear.

Upper chest (Thymus)

Here we find the expression of Higher Will, or God's divine will for us as souls. This Will is more expansive, wiser, and more loving than our smaller personal will in the physical world. Opening this area leads to more awareness of and passion for our unique purpose in this life. A puffed-out and rigid upper chest illustrates a thwarted expression of a person's higher will. Such people don't fully let the breath go.

Affirmations: It is safe to express my will. My will and God's will are one.

Heart area

No breath in this area indicates that the heart is *shut down*, and the expression of love and compassion is closed off. Such people often had willful parents and shut their heart energy down to survive a battle of wills. In this case, forgiveness work is often needed, which we begin by embracing and breathing through the repressed anger, resentment, and grief. The person has been wounded or violated and needs to establish a sense of safety and willingness to open the heart. Once this area opens, the person will be able to receive and give love much more freely and fluidly.

Affirmations: It is safe to open my heart. I am loving. I am lovable. It is safe to receive/express love. It is safe to express my feelings now and always. I deserve only love. I am only love.

Mid-chest area (solar plexus)

Tightness of the sub-sternum muscle indicates fear. The *fear belt* runs across the diaphragm and bottom of the ribs. The upper solar plexus area relates to the fear of letting go—trusting and surrendering. Fluttering of the upper abdomen during breathing indicates the integration of fear patterns. People who puff out this area during breathing are often accustomed to doing everything themselves "to get it right"—a perfectionist who often gets overburdened.

Affirmations: I let go and let God. My heart and will are one. I let it come and let it go. I am always safe.

Abdomen

Here in the lower belly reside personal will and creativity. Abdominal or diaphragmatic breathers are therefore strong-willed, creative people. They are also grounded and comfortable in their bodies. Those who do not breathe into this lower respiratory area have weaker wills and are easily dominated or taken advantage of. They tend to hold onto self-judgment and guilt. They also tend to be unfocused and are generally not fully in their bodies, often describing themselves as feeling spacey and disconnected from their bodies.

Affirmations: It is safe to be in my body. It is easy to breathe. I forgive myself completely. I am perfect creativity.

Appendix B
The Physics of Breathing

By Scott Kwiatkowski, D.O.

Disease develops when there is something wrong with a bodily function—when your body is unable to do the work it usually does. There are many things that can alter how your body works by damaging it. Infections are top on the list. An infection is a multiplication of parasitic organisms inside the body. So when bacteria, viruses, or parasites enter the body there is an infection, and when they grow enough to slow down the body's ability to work, there is disease. Here we will talk about different bacteria that cause infection and why the infections can be fought by increasing the oxygenation in the body.

Bacteria are single-cell organisms that are smaller and more primitive than animal cells. Bacteria are more primitive in that they have less complicated DNA; they lack many of the chemicals animal cells have, and their cells are given shape by a cell wall.

Many bacteria are found naturally inside the body. These rarely cause trouble unless, like weeds in a garden, they become overgrown or grow where they don't belong. Other types of bacteria cause disease whenever they grow in humans. These are referred to as pathological bacteria.

Bacteria can be divided into different groups, depending upon how they use or don't use oxygen to make energy. Some bacteria use air in order to make energy, and are called *aerobic*, while others don't like oxygen at all—called *anaerobic*. Many bacteria can thrive with or without oxygen and are called *facultative anaerobes*.

Aerobic bacteria make certain enzymes (chemicals) so that they can live comfortably where there is oxygen. These enzymes help the bacteria use oxygen to make energy and also to break down the chemicals they don't like that oxygen makes. The anaerobic bacteria use fermentation to make energy and don't have these enzymes. Instead they die when they come in contact with oxygen. Microaerophilic bacteria have only one type of protective enzyme, so they are able to tolerate low amounts of oxygen.

Oxygen molecules are very reactive in that they readily join with other molecules like hydrogen and other oxygen molecules. So, an oxygen molecule (O_2) may lose some charge and become a superoxide radical (O_2). Or it can join with hydrogen and become a hydroxy radical (OH), or it can join with two hydrogen molecules and form hydrogen peroxide (H_2O_2). These chemicals are called *oxygen radicals*, and they are very toxic to a cell, animal or bacterial. They will pull apart a cell membrane or cell wall, piece by piece, by pulling away the molecules that hold it together. This process is a form of oxidation, and the reason aerobic cells are not destroyed is because of antioxidants and enzymes they contain. The enzymes *catalase* and *peroxidase* break down the hydrogen peroxide molecule. The enzyme *superoxide dismutase* (also known as SOD) joins the oxygen radical to two hydrogen molecules, forming hydrogen peroxide and a stable oxygen molecule.

Animal cells, aerobic bacteria, and facultative anaerobes can produce all three enzymes. Microaerophilic bacteria can only produce superoxide dismutase, and can only tolerate low amounts of oxygen. Anaerobic bacteria have none, and therefore die in the presence of oxygen.

Here are some common bacteria that would probably be affected by increased amounts of oxygen in the tissues. Examples of Microaerophilic bacteria include Streptococcus (some species), Spirochetes, Campylobacter, and Helicobacter. While examples of Anaerobic bacteria include Peptostreptococcus, Bacte-roides, and Clostridium.

Campylobacter jejuni: causes a sudden attack of diarrhea with abdominal pain and all over body aches. Humans become infected by animal contact or improperly handled food.

Helicobacter pylori: causes stomach ulcers in humans. Transmission is unknown.

Streptococcus viridans: a large group of strep bacteria that weakly destroy red blood cells. They are normally found in the mouth, vagina, and intestines. However, when the bacteria leaves the mouth and is inhaled (usually with food), it can cause walled off pockets of pus and pneumonia.

Peptostreptococcus: has the same profile as Strep viridans.

Bacteroides fragelis: composes 99% of the intestinal bacteria. It lives peacefully there unless the bowel is perforated by trauma. B. Fragelis then forms abscesses in the tissues outside the bowel.

Bacteroides melanogenicus: normally found in the mouth, but when inhaled, kills lung tissue.

It is common to find these organisms, but rare to find them causing disease. They rarely cause disease because the body is well equipped to fight the infections for the reasons described above. However, there is more to the story.

As you know, there are many things that cause the body to function poorly and result in disease that are not caused from outside invasion of the body. Autoimmune diseases, psychiatric disease, and cancer are good examples. No matter what the cause, the mechanism of cure is still the same. All disease will benefit from improving body motion, circulation, and oxygenation. This is easily accomplished by the act of breathing, but optimally accomplished by Transformational Breathing.

Here is why body motion, circulation, and oxygenation are so important. Everything in your body needs to move, or have something move through it. This goal is accomplished by fluid movement, both inside and outside of your cells. You need a good amount of fluid and mobility in your body to ensure that each cell receives the nutrients and oxygen it needs, the chemicals to repair damage and kill infection, and the ability to remove waste. Think of your kitchen sink. If the water doesn't move through it, you get a backup of gunk, and gunk is very irritating. If you improve the fluid motion through the sink, the gunk is carried away, and the irritation is gone.

Oxygen and other nutrients are carried in your blood, by your arteries, to the cells of your body. These goodies are dumped out of the arteries into the fluid that surrounds the cells. While in that fluid, the nutrients and oxygen float over the cells. Your cells *chow down* and toss the wastes back into the fluid so your veins and lymph vessels can carry the waste away. When any part of this process is disrupted, either the cells won't eat enough or they won't get rid of their waste properly. This means the cells will starve, roll in filth, or both. This is just like what happens at a restaurant. Your waiter brings you your food and puts it on your table. You eat and put your dishes and the stuff you don't eat back on the table. Your waiter or busboy comes back and collect what you left. If you slow down or get rid of any one of these people, you will either be uncomfortably hungry, drown in your dishes, or both. Likewise, the movement of fluid in your body is *critical* to its survival. Now you know the important things motion and circulation do, but how does this relate to breathing?

Oxygen is one of the primary components of air. As you know, it is necessary as a building block and catalyst for most metabolic processes in the body. You also know that oxygen radicals are derived from oxygen and they are necessary for fighting disease. So it is beneficial to have as much air as possible, and, in order to get air into your body, it has to move. To pull air into the lungs, muscles have to contract, pull the ribs upward, and flatten the spine. Full breathing, using all eight diaphragms, will move your entire body with each breath. This breathing creates motion, circulation, and oxygenation for a healthy body.

What exactly does oxygen do for us and why do our bodies need so much of it? The body needs oxygen in order to make energy. The body makes and stores energy in chemical form, mostly in the molecule called ATP (adenosine-tri-phosphate). When ATP is used, one of the phosphates is given away, causing a lot of heat energy. This changes the ATP into ADP (adenosine-*di*-phosphate). The energy that is given off is used to power all the chemical reactions of the body. ATP is like the gas of your car—it makes it go—but it also builds your vehicle, repairs it, and makes more gas. You can see now that oxygen is essential for the body. Here's how:

Again, the body needs oxygen to make energy (ATP). This process of building energy with oxygen is called *aerobic respiration*. The body can also build energy by not using oxygen *(anaerobic respiration)*, and by breaking down sugar. However, these last two are not nearly sufficient to fulfill the body's needs, as demonstrated by the discomfort we feel when we hold our breath.

So how does the body make energy with oxygen? Oxygen is drawn into the lungs by breathing. From the lungs, the oxygen diffuses into the blood. The oxygen is carried, on red blood cells, throughout the body and is released into the tissues. The oxygen then moves inside the individual cells and finds the tiny power-houses of the cell—the mitochondrion. Inside the mitochondrion of the cell, the oxygen becomes a part of the *electron transport chain*.

The electron transport chain is a group of chemicals that function as an assembly line. On this assembly line, oxygen helps pass electrical charge downstream. Moving charge makes power, and this power is used to put a phosphate molecule onto ADP, converting it back into ATP. So oxygen is used on the assembly line to replenish the body's energy! In fact, more than 90% of the oxygen in the body is used for this.

Some chemicals can directly inhibit this process, and they are therefore deemed *poisons*. Carbon monoxide, for example, affects the process by slowing the electron transport chain and making the red blood cells unable to carry new oxygen. Poisoning and death by carbon monoxide is a quick process. Cyanide also affects the electron transport chain directly. By breaking the flow of electrons, cyanide stops it cold, and death happens very fast.

So if hypoxia (lack of oxygen distribution to the cells) is severe, it can cause cell death. But what happens if the body doesn't have enough oxygen? Or isn't able to use what it has on a less dramatic, more chronic basis? In this case, there will be a decrease in mental activity and a decrease in the muscles' ability to do work.

With more oxygen, the body can make more energy. More energy makes all things in the body happen bigger and better. More oxygen means your body can function better, and this can easily translate into more energy and passion in your life.

Something in the Air

We have mentioned that air gets from outside the body to the lungs by breathing. Once in the lungs, the air moves from the upper airways to the end of the air passages, small membranous sacks called alveoli. The alveoli have small blood vessels (capillaries) that form a mesh around them. After the air gets to the alveoli, the oxygen in it must diffuse into these alveolar capillaries. (Diffusion is the passive movement of a substance from high concentration to low concentration). Oxygen moves from the higher concentration in the alveoli to lower concentration in the blood, so that it can be transported to the other body tissues and be used to make energy via cellular respiration.

While we spent so much time talking about how important air was and discussing better ways to get it, we never really talked about what air is. There are many gases in air. Oxygen is the most popular, but it isn't the only one. Since we are concerned about getting more oxygen into our bodies for increased energy, we need to ask, "How much is out there and how much can I get in here?" Another important question to consider is whether we can get too much oxygen and what happens if we do.

Air contains: Oxygen 21%, Nitrogen 78%, Argon 0.93%, Carbon dioxide 0.03%, other minor gases including a variable amount of water vapor (1). The ones we are concerned about in breathing are: oxygen, carbon dioxide, nitrogen, and water.

As stated in Guyton and Hall's *Textbook of Medical Physiology*, 9th Ed., the gases in air have different concentrations outside the lung versus inside the lung. Outside the lung, the relative percentages are listed above. Inside the lung, the air is humidified as it travels to the end portions of the lung, the alveoli, and this water vapor dilutes the other gases. The differences in gas concentrations can also be explained by knowing that alveolar air is only partially replaced with each breath, oxygen is constantly being absorbed from the alveolar air, and carbon dioxide is constantly diffusing into the alveoli. So, due to the extra water vapor, the absorption of oxygen, and the dumping of carbon dioxide, the alveolar gas concentrations are different than atmospheric air.

Alveolar air contains: Oxygen 14%, Nitrogen 75%, Carbon dioxide 5%, and water 6%.

You can get the alveolar oxygen concentration of 14% to approach the atmospheric concentration of 21% with increased breathing, such as during a Transformational Breathing Session. As the rate and volume of breath increases, the oxygen supply increases. This happens because you are getting O_2 to the alveoli faster than it can be taken away in the blood. This will enhance the diffusion of O_2 across the alveolar capillary membrane, resulting in increased amounts in the blood. Increased blood concentration of O_2 results in higher tissue concentrations as well as increased concentrations inside the cell itself.

The increase in blood flow results in more nutrients and oxygen being delivered to the cells, and the removal of CO_2 and other metabolic wastes is also enhanced. The increased amount of O_2 delivery allows the cells to increase their metabolic rate, and produce more energy (ATP). Thus, there is more O_2 in the tissues and more energy production.

Aside from an overall increase in well-being, are there any other effects of increased O_2 in the tissues? Absolutely. As we discussed in the previous section on bacteria, oxygen in its *active* form is very reactive because it readily joins to other molecules like hydrogen and other oxgygen molecules. (1) An oxygen molecule (O_2) may lose some charge and become a superoxide radical (O_2-), join with a hydrogen and become a hydroxy radical (OH-), or join with two hydrogen molecules and form hydrogen peroxide (H_2O_2) (2).

These chemicals are very toxic to a cell, animal, or bacterial. Oxygen and its radicals are in a balance—balanced as if on a seesaw. They freely join together and break apart into consistent proportions (1). By adding more O_2, we drive the process to produce more oxygen radicals in order to maintain the balance. Thus, more hydrogen peroxide, superoxide radicals, and hydroxy radicals will result as O_2 increases (2). Ooh, but aren't radicals bad? Only if they are excessive.

When the production and breakdown of radicals is out of balance, the outcome is poor health. There are harmful effects of too much oxygen, and most of these effects surround a process called *oxygen toxicity*. The process of oxygen toxicity is incompletely understood and poorly defined, but some parameters have been identified (2). There are three variables related to oxygen: the percentage, the pressure, and the exposure time. Increases in these increase the risk for toxicity.

The major symptoms of toxicity are related to the nervous system. Common symptoms include tremors, twitching and convulsions. This does not occur during breathing air (a mixture of gases) at normal atmospheric pressure. This toxicity usually occurs in people who are breathing 50% or greater oxygen at increased pressures, two times atmospheric pressure or more (2,3).

To increase atmospheric pressure above 2 atm, you would have to go 33 feet below sea level or get into a hyperbaric (pressurizing) chamber. Since air contains only 20% oxygen, it is impossible to get more than 20% oxygen from the air while breathing it in at normal atmospheric pressures. Thus, oxygen toxicity is not something that will happen during Transformational Breathing. The normal, healthy cells in our bodies have enzymes to protect against damage from radicals, and it is only when these enzymes are overwhelmed that there is trouble.

So the physiological increase in O_2 achieved by increasing your breathing rate and volume will also increase the radical formation. However, our cells have protective enzymes and are better able to produce them than most bacterial and cancerous cells. Remember that the enzymes *catalase* and *peroxidase* break down the hydrogen peroxide molecule. The enzyme *superoxide dismutase* joins the oxygen radical to two hydrogen molecules, forming hydrogen peroxide and a stable oxygen molecule. This increase in tissue O_2 will aid in the demise of bacteria and cancer cells, while improving the health of our own cells and bodies.

The Physiology of Activation

The symptoms of activation include warmth in the ears, tingling in the palms and soles, sometimes followed by minor tetany. Tetany is most similar to a muscle cramp—a contraction that doesn't release easily. These contractions usually occur in the palms, soles, and around the mouth.

Although the symptoms of activation are similar to those of oxygen toxicity and hyperventilation, neither of these occurs during activation. Hyperventilation can occur during the Transformational Breathing process, although the facilitator watches for it. Breathers can avoid it fairly easily by relaxing as they exhale. Hyperventilation, as defined by Steadman's Medical Dictionary, is an increased breathing rate that results in lowering the concentration of carbon dioxide (CO_2) in the blood. However, the rate of breathing is not the most important component of hyperventilation—the volume of exhaled gas is. In hyperventilation, the exhalation is either longer than the inhalation or it is more forceful. This results in moving more CO_2 out of the blood. Since CO_2 acts as an acid, removing it raises the pH of the blood, making the blood more alkaline (basic). The body functions poorly when the pH is out of the normal range of 7.35 to 7.44.

The later symptoms of hyperventilation are probably not due to a decrease in CO_2, but rather a decrease in N_2, though this remains to be seen. Unlike hyperventilating breathers, whose exhalation is more forceful and voluminous than their inhalation, Transformational Breathers use a conscious, purposeful inhalation and relax on the exhalation, allowing it to happen from the recoil of the inflated structures. Using correct breathing technique, CO_2 is expelled proportionately, no pH change occurs, and hyperventilation does not happen. So, what does happen that will cause activation, if it is not an increase in O_2 or a decrease in CO_2? The most likely answer is a change in the blood's nitrogen concentration.

With good ventilation, as happens during exercise or Transformational Breathing, the alveolar concentration of O_2 almost reaches the atmospheric concentration of O_2. The increasing O_2

molecules in the alveoli displace the N_2 molecules. Since more O_2 molecules are present, more diffuse into the blood, and more N_2 is displaced there as well. Nitrogen gas acts as an anesthetic. The higher the concentration of gas, the less excitable is a neuron (a nerve cell) (2,3). This is most easily seen during deep sea diving, and the process is called *nitrogen narcosis*. As a diver's depth increases, the amount of N_2 increases proportionately in their blood. As the amount of N_2 increases beyond the normal range, neurological symptoms develop (1). The symptoms range from giddiness and clumsiness with low exposure, to muscle weakness and stupor with massive exposure (1).

Since N_2 acts as an anesthetic/depressant, it stands to reason that removing the neuronal depressant will lead to increased neuronal excitability. This means that as O_2 concentration increases in the alveoli, blood, and tissue, the N_2 concentration will decrease in these areas, allowing the tissue to become more easily energized and excitable. This is what happens during activation— tissue becomes easily excitable. Muscle tissue becomes more excitable, allowing contractions to occur more easily, and "tetany" sometimes occurs. Nerve fibers also become more excitable, fire more easily, and body tingling is perceived.

Thus, by looking at a well-studied model for neuronal depression (increased N_2 concentrations in deep-sea diving) it is easy to see how neuronal excitability could be enhanced by decreasing N_2 concentrations. This decrease in N_2 concentration is the most likely mechanism for activation during Transformational Breathing, rather than an increase in O_2 or a decrease in CO_2.

Admittedly, this theory probably does not address the whole picture, but it does offer a solid physiological explanation for activation. There are other explanations for activation that are more metaphysical in nature, and perhaps equally valid. One explanation describes bringing in more Prana (Life Force) with increased breathing. This increase in Prana may also be responsible for activation as well as the other healthful effects of Transformational Breathing.

Dr. Kwiatkowski's specialty is in functional anatomy—how the body works, how it becomes diseased—and hands-on manipulative treatments for restoring good health. Dr. Kwiatkowski attended Potsdam College and was awarded a degree in Honors Psychology, a research-intensive program emphasizing neuroanatomy. He later worked for the University at Albany, where he assisted a team researching neurotransmitters in the brain and retina. Immediately prior to medical school, Dr. Kwiatkowski attended Stillpoint Center for Massage and became a licensed massage therapist. During the training he extensively studied functional anatomy, myology, and kinesiology. Dr. Kwiatkowski obtained his medical degree from the New York College of Osteopathic Medicine in 1998, and worked at St. Barnabas Hospital, Department of Osteopathic Manipulative Medicine. Upon completion of his residency, he became certified specialist in the fields of Neuro-Musculoskeletal Medicine and Osteopathic Manipulation. He now lives and heads his holistic medical practice in Bethesda, MD.

References for this appendix

1. Guyton, Hall. *Textbook of Medical Physiology, 9th Ed.* WB Saunders Co., Philadelphia, 1996, pp. 501-513, 557-559.

2. Scanlon, CL., Spearman, CB., Sheldon, RL. *Egan's Fundamentals of Respiratory Care, 6th Ed.* Mosby, St. Louis, 1995, pp. 704-707.

3. Murray, JF., Nadel, JA., *Textbook of Respiratory Medicine, 2nd Ed.* WB Saunders Co., Philadelphia, 1996, pp. 2108-2109.

4. Miller-Keane. *Encyclopedia and Dictionary of Medicine, Nursing, and Allied Health, 6th Ed.* WB Saunders Co., Philadelphia, 1997, pg 785.

Appendix C
Bibliography

Altman, Nathaniel; *Oxygen Healing Therapies for Optimum Health and Vitality*; Healing Arts Press, Vermont, 1995.

Bradshaw, John; *Healing the Shame that Binds You*

Cousins, Norman; *Anatomy of An Illness; As Perceived by the Patient*; W.W. Norton and Company, Inc., New York, 1979.

Douglas-Klotz, Neil; *Prayers of the Cosmos*, Thorsons/ Harper San Francisco.

Dyer, Wayne M.D.; *Your Erroneous Zones*

Ellis, George; *The Breath Of Life, Mastering The Breathing Techniques of Pranayama*, Newcastle Publishing, California, 1993.

Farhi, Donna; *The Breathing Book: Good Health and Vitality Through Essential Breath Work*; Henry Holt and Company, Inc., New York, 1996.

Foundation for Inner Peace; *A Course In Miracles,* 1971.

Grof, Stanislav, MD; *The Holotropic Mind; The Three Levels of Human Consciousness and How They Shape Our Lives.* Harper Collins, New York, 1990.

Keyes, Ken Jr.; *The Hundredth Monkey,* Vision Books, Kentucky, 1981.

McCabe, Edward; *Oxygen Therapies; A New Way of Approaching Disease.* Energy Publications, New York, 1988.

Milanovich, Dr. Norma J.; *We, The Arcturians: A True Experience,* Athena Publishing, 1990.

Rama, Ballantine and Hymes; *Science of Breath: A Practical Guide,* Himalayan Institute Press, Pennsylvania, 1979.

Szekely, Edmond Bordeaux; *The Essene Gospel of Peace,* International Biogenic Society, B.C. Canada, 1981.

Schreiber, Flora Rheta; *Sybil,* Warner Books, 1995.

Appendix D
Recommended Reading List

Baba, Prem Raja; *The God Book: Create Your Own Miracles*, Prem Raja Baba, CA, 1998.

Baba, Prem Raja; *The Joy Book: Ascension, Life Mastery, Unconditional Love,* Prem Raja Baba, CA, 1991.

Byron, Katie, with Steven Michael; *Loving What Is,* Harmony Books, New York, NY , 2002.

Chopra, Deepak, M.D.; *Ageless Body Timeless Mind: A Quantum Alternative To Growing Old,* Harmony Books, a division of Crown Publishers, Inc., NY, 1993.

Clark and Martine; *Health, Youth, and Beauty Through Color Breathing*, Berkley Medallion Books, California, 1977.

Epstein, Donald M., with Nathaniel Altman; *The 12 Stages of Healing: A Network Approach To Wholeness,* co-published by Amber-Allen Publishing and New World Library, CA, 1994.

Hay, Louise L.; *You Can Heal Your Life,* Hay House, Inc., CA, 1984.

Jasmuheen; *Living On Light: The Source of Nourishment for the New Millennium,* KOHA Publishing, Germany, 1998.

Johari, Harish; *Breath, Mind, and Consciousness*, Destiny Books, Vermont, 1989.

Jon, Shahan; *Receiving The Cosmic Christ: The Experience of Global Community*, Karuna Foundation, CA, 1990.

Jones, Laurie Beth; *Jesus CEO: Using Ancient Wisdom for Visionary Leadership*, Hyperion, NY, 1992.

Kelder, Peter; *Ancient Secret of the Fountain of Youth*, Doubleday, New York, 1985.

Lewis, Dennis; *The Tao Of Natural Breathing: For Health, Well-Being and Inner Growth*, Mountain Wind Publishing, California, 1997.

Matheson, Richard; *What Dreams May Come*, Tom Doherty Associates, Inc., NY, 1978.

Nhat Hanh, Thich; *Breathe! You Are Alive: Sutra on the Full Awareness of Breathing,* Parallax Press, California,1996.

Nishino, Kozo; *The Breath Of Life, Using the Power of Ki for Maximum Vitality*, Kodansha International, New York, 1997.

Price, John Randolph; *The Abundance Book,* Hay House, Inc., CA, 1987.

Ramacharaka, Yogi; *The Hindu Yogi: Science Of Breath,* D. B. Taraporevala Sons and Co., Private Ltd., Bombay, India, 1966.

Ray, Sondra, with Bob Mandel; *Birth and Relationship: How Your Birth Affects Your Relationships*, Celestial Arts, CA, 1987.

Redfield, James; *The Tenth Insight: Holding The Vision,* Warner Books, Inc., NY, 1996.

Sieczka, Helmut G.; *Chakra Breathing, Pathway to Energy, Harmony and Self-Healing,* published by Life Rhythm, California, 1993.

Sky, Michael; *Breathing: Expanding Your Power and Energy,* Bear and Company, Inc., New Mexico, 1990.

Walsch, Neale Donald; *Conversations With God: An Uncommon Dialogue, Book 2*, Hampton Roads Publishing Company, Inc., VA, 1997.

Weil, M.D., Andrew; *Spontaneous Healing: How To Discover and Enhance Your Body's Natural Ability to Maintain and Heal Itself,* Alfred A. Knopf, Inc., NY, 1995.

Weil, MD., Andrew: *Breathing, The Master Key to Self Healing,* Audio, Sounds True, Boulder ,CO., 1999

Ford, Debbie: *The Dark Side of The Light Chasers, Reclaiming Your Power, Creativity, Brilliance and Dreams,* Riverhead Books, New York, 1998.

Appendix E
Transformationa Breath Facilitators

Please check our current website breathe2000.com for a current llisting of facilitators and programs.

Please note: *This section is organized alphabetically by U.S. state or name of the country (if outside the U.S.). For example, look up the state of Maine because it is in the USA. But if you want to find a facilitator in the province of New Brunswick in Canada, look it up under Canada.*

ARKANSAS
Ed Ashmead, Graduate
Eagle River, AK
907-694-7817
eashmead@gci.net

ARIZONA
Karen Connelly, CTBF
Tucson, AZ
520-878-9047

BELGIUM
Catherine Malburg, CTBF
Herve Belgium
32 87 67 53 41
sacrednest@freegates.be

Sylvio Malburg, CTBF
Herve Belgium
32 87 67 53 41
sacrednest@freegates.be

CALIFORNIA
George Aiken, MA CTBF
Santa Rosa, CA
800-488-6078
gaiken@georgeaiken.com

Robin Almaas, Graduate
San Diego CA
858-693-3367 / 858-922-6891

Sophia Arise, Trainer
San Francisco Bay CA
415-924-6333
sophiaarise@yahoo.com

Rainbow Casey, MD DD CTBF
Desert Hot Springs CA
760-251-5000
healthcoach@usa.net

Alison Coppola, CTBF
Newbury Park CA
805-480-0427
acoppola@earthlink.net

Diane Crouch, Graduate
Alpine CA
619-445-7440
DivinneInsprAne@aol.com

Robert Crouch, Graduate
Alpine CA
619-445-7444
BonesZone6@aol.com

Gail Darwin, CST CTBF
Los Angeles CA
310-375-6892
gail@earthhealing.com

Melinda Dewey, Trainer
Costa Mesa CA
714-662-5561
melindadewey@earthlink.net

Darrell Franklin, CTBF
Palm Springs CA
760-321-0079
obawizard@aol.com

Bobby Glicksir, CTBF
Santa Ana CA
714-973-7860

Sandi Gune, CTBF
Desert Hot Springs CA
760-251-2583 / 760-251-2583
rgune@aol.com

Kathleen Israel, CTBF
San Diego CA
619-287-0240 / 619-287-9021
KIGDESIGN@aol.com

Ron Israel, Graduate
San Diego CA
619-287-0240 / 619-287-9021
iamturtleman@msn.com

Mikela Veronika Jeffmar, CTBF
Santa Cruz CA
831-464-8542
veronika@cruzio.com

Jessica Leaf, Trainer
Southern CA
760-724-9393 / 760-724-6006
breathe_now@webtv.net

Judy Lin, Trainer
Los Angeles CA
909-865-0600

Bill Mayo, CTBF
Seal/Huntington Beach CA
562-596-9107
wtmayo@ieee.org

Rick Nichols, Graduate
Escondido CA
760-728-7317
rick or pat
@www.heartinspired.com

Domani Osborne, CoTrainer
San Diego CA
858-277-1885

Marilyn Perona, CTBF
Orange County CA
949-855-4695
laughingdancer3@yahoo.com

Rehanna Rich, CTBF
Palm Desert CA
760-568-1230

Wendy Rudell, Trainer
San Diego CA
619-589-4716 / 619-405-4990
wendyr@optimumhealth.org

Shelley Salvatore, CTBF
Nevada City CA
530-470-1081

Bonnie Selva, CTBF
San Diego CA
866-654-3734 / 619-464-5295
soul2soltravel@nethere.com

Karen Louise Sisson, CTBF
Huntington Beach CA
714-840-1353

Douglas Snow, CTBF
Half Moon Bay CA
650-906-4799

Roger Wanderscheid, CTBF
Joshua Tree CA
760-366-1017

Annette White, CoTrainer
San Diego CA
858-693-3367
annetteewhite@hotmail.com

Maryann Zimmermann,
CoTrainer
San Diego CA
858-488-1921
joylove2@aol.com

We Care Health Center
Desert Hot Springs CA
800-888-2523 / 760-251-2261
www.wecarespr.care

CANADA
Phyllis Carson, Graduate
Riverview NB Canada
pcarson@nbnet.nb.ca

Catherine Doucette, CTBF
Saint John NB Canada
506-652-9915
cathd@nbnet.nb.ca

Joyce Doucette, CTBF
Rothesay NB Canada
506-847-8119
joyceid@nb.sympatico.ca

200

COLORADO
Allison Howard, CTBF
Lafayette CO
303-666-6864

Pat McLaurin, CTBF
Boulder CO
303-546-0535
joybliss@aol.com

Danae Shanti, CTBF
Boulder CO
303-530-3920
www.soundingfree.net

Dyan Stein, CTBF
Durango CO
970-382-9939
alyvianactivations@sisna.com

CONNECTICUT
Beth U. Udoma, M.A.
"Peaches" (Trainer)
203-261-8813 / 203-558-1598
inlovingbreath@yahoo.com

Carol Christmas, Graduate
New Haven CT
203-281-0345
jb.cc@juno.com

Owen Coffey, Graduate
New Haven CT
203-787-1383
owencoffey@hotmail.com

Lois Como-Grasso, CTBF
West Hartford CT
860-747-3999
loisgrasso@sbcglobal.com

Andonia Dakis, CTBF
Branford CT
203-488-7090 / 203-488-7090
andonia@snet.net

Darah Homewood, Graduate
Greenwich CT
203-637-4283
darahhomewood@earthlink.com

Carol Piro, CTBF
Norwalk CT
203-866-3264 / 203-554-8433
carol@aromapersona.com

Roberta Scaglione, Trainer
Branford, CT
203-483-5568
rms220@hotmail.com

Cynthia Van Savage, CTBF
Ridgefield CT
203-438-1022

Dr.Timothy Ross, Graduate
Whelan, MA. DC
Thomaston CT
860-283-5171

ENGLAND
Pamela Ansell, CTBF
London England
011 207 731 5560
pamelaansell@lineone.net

Sarah Clifton, CTBF
Norwich England
01603-631391
sarah190@talk21.com

Max Delli Guanti, Trainer
London England
44 18 1441 9659
Maxhealed@aolcom

Teri Gregory, Graduate
Norfolk England
44 0 1603 750075

Chris Halliday Graduate
Yorkshire England
011 1422 846318
cjhalliday@lycos.co.uk

Ange Leake, Trainer
Derbyshire, England
011441629824023
ange_tbuk@hotmail.com

Susan Seely, CTBF
Norwich, England
011441 60 366 1773
susan.seely@virgin.net

Jackie Turner CTBF
W. Midlands, England
011441215504234

FLORIDA
Brian Boggs, CTBF
Ft. Lauderdale FL
954-452-7352
brianboggs@juno.com

Linda Boone, CTBF
West Palm Beach FL
561-433-3215
whippetdoc@aol.com

Gaia Budhai, Trainer
Miami Beach FL
305-538-7073 / 305-534-9807
community@synergyyoga.org

Carol Crislip, CTBF
Jenson Beach FL
772-334-7741
crisgardern@msn.com

Denise Dallas, CTBF
Boca Raton FL
516-362-6134

Alina Guttierrez, CTBF
Miami FL
305 273 6650 / 305-669-1989
enrichmg@bellsouth.net

Pat Hill, Graduate
Jacsonville FL
904-389-9239

Audrey Hull, CTBF
Ft. Pierce, FL
561-439-0290 / 772 489 0290
audhull@adelphia.net

Pia Leaman, Graduate
West Palm Beach FL
561-744-1395

Holly Martinez, CTBF
Palm City FL
561-223-9678
Hollybeing@earthlink.net

Pat McLaurin CTBF
Bonita Springs FL
941-992-9409
joybliss@aol.com

Daniel Murray, CTBF
Jenson Beach FL
561-334-0308
danielmurray@hotmail.com

Renida Tai, CTBF
N. Miami FL
877-259-1860
needatai@aol.com

Mary Thixton, CTBF
Palm City FL
561-219-4362

Ed Thrall, CTBF
So. Florida FL
954-629-6633
thrall22@attbi.com

Paul Toliuszis, CTBF
Miami Beach FL
305-534-0374
yogaforgolf72@hotmail.com

GEORGIA
Peg Watkins, CTBF
Dahlonega GA
706-864-2723
pwatkin1@alltel.net

GERMANY
Felicitas Lacueva, CTBF
Ketsch,Germany
49 620 260 5809
transbreath2000@yahoo.com

HAWAII
Gail Longhi, CTBF
Lahaina, Maui HI
808-661-6612
Breathwithtahina@aol.com

ITALY
AchilleBaronioGraduate
Visano, Italy
0139 995 8235
achillebaronio@hotmail.com

Arianna Bitti, Graduate
Piane di Falerone, Italy
01139339 24 70 908
b.farfy@mailcity.com

Francesco Bordino, CTBF
Neive, Italy
01139328 68 61 923
fire.francy@tiscalinet.it

AlessandraCardinCTBF
Vigonza, Italy
0113949 89 31 549
ale@goosepimples.com

Mariagrazia Catalano
Trainer,
Milan, Italy
011392 76 02 0585
merigreis@liberio.it

Mariella Cirlinci, CTBF
Milan, Italy
01139 2 47 32 45
cirlinci@tin.it

Massimo Cirlinci CTBF
Milan, Italy
0113902 47 3245
cirlinci@tin.it

Licia Consuella, Trainer
Milan, Italy
01139 348 5600501
licia@goosepimples.com

Alba Cristiano, CTBF
Chiaravalle C. le Italy
01139 338 348 744
albanascente@albanas
cente.com

Max DamioliTrainer
Milan, Italy
01139 348 560 0501
max@goosepimples.com

Vincenzo DiBonaventura,CTBF
S.Bendetto d/Tronto, Italy
01139338 1042523

PieraFormichini, CTBF
Florence, Italy
01139555004561
piera38@hotmail.com

StefaniaGottardi, Graduate
Pavia, Italy
01139340 30 78 044

Melanie Gueneau, Graduate
Switzerland
guenomel@yahoo.com

Maria Grazia Lenzi, CTBF
Florence, Italy
1139 055 68 08 187
babajaga@iol.it

Rita Massarenti CTBF
Milan, Italy
02 57 60 70 53
rmassarenti@tiscalinet.i

Franco Padovan, Grad
011 39 80 54 22 602
franco.padovan@sacc

Rosanna Petrini, CTBF
Comano, Italy
0041 9194 19749

Nicola Riva, CTBF
Milan, Italy
0113924 802 2795
nik@goosepimples.com

Vittorio Rossi, Graduate
Trento, Italy
vitrossi@hotmail.com

Indalecia Ziett, Graduate
Milan, Italy
011 390 23 15 003
indaleciaziett@hotmail.com

MAINE
Ann Kilby Graduate
Cape Elizabeth, ME
207-799-1699
annkilby@hotmail.com

Andie Locke, CBTF
Poland, ME
207-998-2890
alocke@pivot.net

LaShell Moon, CTBF
Portland, ME
207-854-1627
lashellmoon@aol.com

Donna Packard, CTBF
York Harbor, ME
207-363-1925
donnapackard@aol.com

Tracy Pozzy, CTBF
Bangor, ME
207-947-5972 / 207-942-4117
spirituspoz_@hotmail.com

Colleen Taylor-Copano, CTBF
New Gloucester, ME
207-926-3203
bldrbrook@aol.com

Paul Weiss, Graduate
Bar Harbor, ME
207-288-4128

Laurence Craig-Green, CTBF
Orlando, ME
207-469-6224
fireguy@angelfire.com

MASSACHUSETTS
Linda Benoit, CTBF
Haverhill, MA
978-372-2933
lbenoit47@aol.com

Apara Borrowes, M.S., CTBF
Arlington, MA
781-643-3955

Robert Copeland, Trainer
Springfield MA
413-543-2118
robtcopeland@yahoo.com

Jeffrey Corbett, CTBF
Attleboro MA
508-222-5710

Davio Danielson, CTBF
Plainfield, MA
888-646-3686
davio@ninemtn.com

Brad Foye, CTBF
Concord MA
978-318-9803

Sandra Franconi CTBF
Cape Cod MA
508-385-9035
sandrafranconi@webtv.net

Julia French, CTBF
Beverly MA
978-922-1723
jfrenchdc@earthlink.net

FlorenceGaia, CTBF
Newburyport MA
978-462-5879
fgaia@shore.net

Gail Heinrich, LMT, CTBF
Sharon,MA
781-784-1232

Bethony Howard, CTBF
Holliston MA
508-429-9200 / 508-317-7053
bethanyhow@juno.com

Marcia Kadish, Graduate
Malden, MA
781-321-3377
heart2heart@attglobal.net

Karen K.Keefe, PhD, CTBF,
Lancaster MA
978-368-3338

Judy LaValle, CTBF
Upton MA
508-529-6177
jalavallee@charter.net

Rob Leavitt, CTBF
Fitchburg, MA
978-345-7799
rdleavitt56@hotmail.com

Linda Lennon-Elfman,CTBF
Foxboro MA
508-543-0764

Tanya McCloskey, CTBF
Malden MA
781-321-7733
tanya@bodyworksbest.com

Susan Phipps, CTBF
Wimington MA
598-423-6886
suephipps@aol.com

Samvedam Randles, CTBF,
Watertown, MA
617-926-1301

Tony Reis, Graduate
Beverly, MA
978-921-5406

Mary Shaffer, CTBF
Melrose, MA
617-662-9104

Maura Shannon, CTBF
Natick, MA
508-653-9008
mlshannon1@juno.com

Elaine Squitiero, CTBF
Leominster, MA
978-534-5982
marrrastm@cs.com

MARYLAND
Scott Kwiatkowski, D.O., CTBF
Bethesda, MD
301-718-3696
www.dowellness.com

MEXICO
Eugenia Guzman, CTBF
Cancun, Mexico
telwebcaribe@net.mx

NORTH CAROLINA
Lani Busbin, CTBF
Charlotte, NC
704-365-3080
geww@bellsouth.net

Binji Elder, CTBF
Ashville NC
828-669-9343

Dr. Janet Leslie Orion, D.C.
Trainer
Asheville, NC
828-254-1120
getDrJanet@msn.com

Robin MacCurdy, CTBF
Asheville, NC
828-628-2142
rubymt23@aol.com

NETHERLANDS
Carla Beljaars, CTBF
Stramproy Netherlands
01131 49 556 4023
henk.carla@wxs.nl

Henk Beljaars, CTBF
Stramproy Netherlands
01131 49 556 4023
henk.carta@wxs.nl

Brigette Brandon, CTBF
Zevenaar Netherlands
01131 34 390 206
brigettevos@hotmail.com

Ellis Buis, CTBF
Oss, Netherlands
31 41 262 6511
ebuis@wxs.nl

Peter Dalmeyer, CTBF
Weert, Netherlands
011 31 49 545 1251
011 31 65 534 3772
dalmeijer@linn.nl

Daniel Horne, CTBF
Amsterdam, Netherlands
shekhar@happyyogi

Paul Lenferink, CTBF
Sitard, Netherlands
01131-464-111-588
lenferink@linn.nl

Loes Mulder, CTBF
Nieuwegein, Netherlands
01131 30 605 0143
loes.tdo@bigfoot.com

Cor Poels, CTBF
Reuver, Netherlands
31 77 474 4531
c.poels@ecc.nl

NEW HAMPSHIRE
Bonnie Ainsworth, Graduate
Freedom, NH
603-539-4360
boninjoy@yahoo.com

Anna Champagne, CTBF
Keene, NH
603-358-5133
anglianna@yahoo.com

Elizabeth Comeau, CTBF
Seacoast, NH
603-335-0804
writer33@metrocast.net

Carolyn Cooper-Kelly, Grad
Concord/Laconia NH
603-286-4956
rippleeffects@cyberporta.net

Don Fecteau, CTBF
Laconia NH
603-527-1622
don.fecteau@verizon.com

Larry Johnson, Graduate
Mt. Washington Valley NH
603-367-8068
ljohnson@nh.adelphia.net

Rox Lindbert, Trainer
MA & NH
617-522-3160 / 603-284-9291
r_lindbert@hotmail.com

Rebecca McCormack, Graduate
Lakes Region, NH
603-284-9248

Debby McLean, CTBF
Bedford, NH
603-471-2969

Judy Tache, CTBF
Derry, NH
603 434-2264

NEW JERSEY
Tosho Bailey, Graduate
Lincroft, NJ
732-212-1260
tosho-bailey@usa.net

Michelle DeRose, Graduate
Avalon, NJ
609-465-5079
gaijinrzr@aol.com

Marlise Fesco-Siracusa, CTBF
Margate, NJ
702-257-2857
mnm398@aol.com

Nesrin Kilic, CTBF
Hoboken, NJ
201-798-3222

Julie Mackert, CTBF
Central & North NJ
908-403-9183
julmac2000@yahoo.com

Kathy Smith, CTBF
Somerspoint , NJ
609-601-9272

Shana Waldo, CTBF
So. Jersey, NJ
609-399-0790 / 609-391-0600
shana_blueray@yahoo.com

Steven Zaid, CTBF
Pleasantville, NJ
609-484-8670

NEVADA
Marlise Fesco-Siracusa, CTBF
Las Vegas, NV
702-257-2857
mnm398@aol.com

NEW YORK
Tammy Baker, CTBF
Ithaca, NY
607-273-2076
TLB18@cornell.edu

Lillian Brown Gold, Graduate
New York, NY
201-968-0305
powerhousegold@cs.com

Dr. Janine Burns, CTBF
Huntington Station, NY
516-909-0103
janine@mindspring.com

Carol Hawk, Trainer
Ithaca, NY
607-768-2618
hawk@lightlink.com

Jonathan Morgenstern, Grad
Larchmont, NY
914-834-5263
mjonathanm@aol.com

Jacqueline Moss, CTBF
E. Long Island, NY
631-653-5174
jacmoss@optonline.net

Charyl Ozkaya, Trainer
Long Island, NY
631-723-0029 / 516-532-7633
chozkaya@aol.com

Ms. Parvati, CTBF
Brooklyn, NY
718-833-6720
parvati4@aol.com

Anthony Sainz, Trainer
New York, NY
212-452-7025
asainz@hunter.cuny.edu

Colleen Thornton, Graduate
Tupper Lake, NY
518-359-3898 / 888-273-8841

Lorna Tobin, Co-Trainer
Long Island, NY
516-769-1597
lornabreathe@hotmail.com

Judy Wilson, RN, HNC, CTBF
Nyack & NYC, NY
845-353-7823
judyrn@spyral.net

Chih-ching Wu, Trainer
New York, NY
917-584-7812
chingz@aol.com

OHIO
Mary Schoen, Trainer
Cincinatti, OH
513-533-9749
wconcepts@eos.net

OREGON
Larry Keele, Graduate
Portland, OR
503-992-0600
calmwatersessentials@earthlink.net

Gina Lawrence, CTBF
Portland, OR
503-992-0600
calmwatersessentials@earthlink.com

Margaret Townsend, CTBF
Portland OR
503-635-2981

PENNSYLVANIA
Laura Jensen, CTBF
Huntington Valley, PA
215-914-2194
laurabreathing@yahoo.com

Joan Thirion, CTBF
Bethel, PA
610-867-2523
www.yogaandhealth.com

SAUDI ARABIA
Nora Abdul, CTBF
Al-khobar, Saudi Arabia
966 54 584 0807
breathing_4_life@hotmail.com

SOUTH CAROLINA
Patricia Dase, Graduate
Greenville SC
864-370-2411

Sara Firestone, Trainer
Charleston, SC
843-762-2484
sarafirei@juno.com

Paula Johnson, CTBF
Charleston, SC
843-971-7770 / 843-856-2777
paulaj@awod.com

SWITZERLAND
Isabel Contreras, CTBF
Geneva, Switzerland
33 45 041 4598
00 41 79 397 9115
lifemotivations@aol.com

Carolee Kingsbury, CTBF
Meinier, Switzerland
011 22 752 4951
carolee69@hotmail.com

VERMONT
Joanie Blaxter, Graduate
Brattleboro VT
802-257-5074 / 802-451-1356
jemma@together.net

Vera Riley, Co-Trainer
Brattleboro, VT
802-257-1678 / 802-579-7094
verariley@hotmail.com

Leigh Russell, CTBF
Brattleboro VT
802-254-4184
leighgate@hotmail.com

WASHINGTON
Dave Merrill, CTBF
Seattle WA
206-2361-9875
merrillize@hotmail.com

Millie Stultz, Graduate
Bremerton WA
360-479-2184

WISCONSIN
Gail Corse, CTBF
Euclaire WI
715 878 9709
gcorse@yahoo.com

Special Introductory Offer
with purchase of this book

Order your free copy of *100 Breaths to Joy* on cassette tape, as well as other helpful titles listed below at special discounted prices for the first of each item. Second or more items can also be ordered at the regular price listed. Please indicate the number of each item desired in the space provided.

Orders for Special Introductory Prices can only be placed using this original order form taken from the book and mailed back to the Transformational Breath Foundation. Thank you for supporting the expansion of our work across the globe.

Discount prices for first item. Regular prices for additional quantities.
_____ *100 Breaths to Joy* Cassette - FREE (Regularly $6.00)
_____ *Breathe Deep, Laugh Loudly* Book- $14.00 (Reg $16.95)
_____ *Passion & Power for Living* Video - $22.00 (Reg $24.95)
_____ *Guided Breath Session* Cassette - $10.00 (Reg $12.00)

_____ *Transformational Breathing Guided Session* - CD…Combines the brief *100 Breaths to Joy* introduction and 5-minute breathing meditation, along with the uplifting 45-minute guided breathing session.
Special $15.00   Regularly $18.00

Product Subtotal $ _____

Shipping & Handling $_____ 10% of total ($6.00 min)

Total Due $_____

Name_____

Street Address _____

City_____ State_____

Zip_____

_____ Check or M.O. payable to: *Transformational Breath Foundation* is enclosed.

_____ Charge this order to my card (circle one): AMEX VISA M/C Discover

Card #_____ Exp._____

Signature: _____

Please mail this form, along with your payment to:

Transformational Breath Foundation PO Box 313, Center Sandwich, NH 03227

~ Additional orders may be made by phone: 1-877.4.1.BREATH / 603.284.9291
~ Or online at: www.breathe2000.com